GENDER EQUALITY AND WOMEN EMPOWERMENT

VISION AND CONTRIBUTION OF BABASAHEB DR. B.R. AMBEDKAR

DR. KULDEEP SINGH

Made with ♥ on the Notion Press Platform
www.notionpress.com

Dedicated to the Champions of Women Rights and Harbingers of Social Justice mainly social revolutionaries Jyotiba Phule, Savitribai Phule and Babasaheb Dr. B.R. Ambedkar, my parents and my teachers.

Contents

Foreword

Babasaheb Dr. Ambedkar was a brilliant scholar, a great philosopher, a symbol of knowledge, a pioneer of egalitarian society and social justice, and India's most influential feminist thinker and a strong advocate of gender equality, women's emancipation and empowerment. Along with being the chief architect of the Indian Constitution, he was an excellent economist, a wonderful jurist, an amazing intellectual, a social revolutionary, a thinker of enormous potential and a brilliant speaker. He was a very sensitive humanist and social worker who strongly advocated equal rights for the oppressed, the deprived and women. He expressed and agitated intellectual issues and sentiments by influencing interdisciplinary perspectives along with practical analysis of social and political situations through his writings and speeches. His writings reveal a deep sense of justice and liberation for the people of the deprived class.

The current President Mrs. Draupadi Murmu credited Babasaheb Dr. Ambedkar for her rise to the post of President of India. Highlighting the outstanding contribution made by Dr. Ambedkar for women empowerment and the downtrodden and deprived sections of society, President Smt. Draupadi Murmu, while speaking at the 10th Convocation of Babasaheb Bhimrao Ambedkar University (BBAU), Lucknow, said that Dr. Bhimrao Ambedkar is like God to her and she is here because of him. She said that it was a proud moment for her to address the students at the convocation of the university named after Babasaheb. President Murmu said, "Dr. Bhimrao Ambedkar did something that made me stand before you today."

Babasaheb Dr. Ambedkar not only devoted his life to improving the conditions of the underprivileged sections of the society, but as a true nationalist, he also made great efforts for the unity and integrity of the country. His ideas on coordination and 'Samajik Samrasata' continued to inspire the efforts for national integration. As India's most ardent well-wisher of women, he played a remarkable and incomparable role, which has been attempted to be highlighted through this book. It is hoped that this book will not only acquaint readers with his feminist ideas and the steps taken by Dr. Ambedkar for women empowerment as a social activist, labor minister, constitution maker and law minister, but will also work to provide contemporary relevance to his egalitarian and inclusive ideas.

Preface

Generally, Babasaheb Dr. Bhimrao Ramji Ambedkar is world renowned as the architect of the Indian Constitution and also known for his wisdom and struggle for the emancipation of the underprivileged, but he also made a very significant, amazing and incomparable contribution for the welfare of women, which is enough to call him a true feminist. This book, GENDER EQUALITY AND WOMEN EMPOWERMENT: VISION AND CONTRIBUTION OF BABASAHEB DR. B.R. AMBEDKAR is based on my another book, *Mahila Adhikaron ke Liye Dr. Ambedkar Ka Yogdaan*, which is in Hindi language. Indeed, this is a translated and slightly modified form of my above mentioned book. In this book, an attempt is being made to highlight the remarkable vision and role of Dr. B.R. Ambedkar as a great feminist and a strong advocate and true warrior of women empowerment. Through this book, an attempt has been made to give a suitable answer to the question, what did Babasaheb Dr. B.R. Ambedkar do for women in India?

As we all know that the world has been almost male dominated. All over the world, women were confined to the domestic sphere, while public life was reserved for men. In the world, there was patriarchy dominance and the social, economic and political condition of women was very pathetic. They were condemned to live a life of exploitation, deprivation, humiliation and oppression. And all this was due to their own people whose discriminatory behavior made women suffer. As far as rights are concerned, they had zero rights and certainly no political rights. In medieval Europe, women were denied the right to own property, study or take part in public life. In France in the late 19th century, women were forced to cover their heads in public, and in some parts of Germany, a husband had the right to sell his wife. Women had neither social equality nor the political right to vote. To get them out of such a humiliating situation, many thinkers and activists came forward who are called feminists. To combat this pitiable condition of women, feminist ideas started taking shape mainly in the western world.

As far as India is concerned, women experienced a bitter life compared to other parts of the world as they were not only deprived of freedom and equality but were also forced to burn themselves along with the dead body of their husband. Women were trapped in the web of cruel and disgusting traditions. Widows were not allowed to remarry even if they had lost their spouses in childhood. Girl child education was completely prohibited and educating a girl or women was considered a sin. Child marriage and female foeticide were also very heinous social evils prevalent in India. They got no rights except duties.

In India too, many feminist thinkers and activists came forward in support of women rights and women empowerment, which mainly included Mahatma Jyotiba Phule, Savitribai Phule, Fatima Sheikh, Babasaheb Dr. Ambedkar and Dr. Ram Manohar Lohia. In this book, the vision of Babasaheb Dr. B.R. Ambedkar regarding women emancipation and his contribution for women empowerment is being highlighted. It is hoped that through this book, readers, especially women, will get acquainted with the thinking of Dr. Ambedkar and his great contribution for women empowerment and they will get an opportunity to express their gratitude to women benefactor Babasaheb Dr. Ambedkar.

Dr. Kuldeep Singh
Lecturer-Political Science
GMSSSS, Sector-55
Faridabad

Acknowledgements

Feminist thinkers and activists made notable efforts to emancipate women globally. In India too, many feminist thinkers and activists came forward in support of women's rights and their empowerment, including great men and thinkers like Mahatma Jyotiba Phule, Savitribai Phule, Fatima Sheikh, Babasaheb Dr. Ambedkar and Dr. Ram Manohar Lohia, who raised a strong voice for women's interests as a struggling warrior. In this book, the role played by Dr. Ambedkar especially for women empowerment is being highlighted. I bow down to Babasaheb Dr. Ambedkar and all feminists and warriors of social justice and express my gratitude to all those scholars and writers from whose works I have obtained important information and prepared this book with relevant analysis.

This book is based on secondary resources of research. That is, relevant information has been collected from various books and websites in the creation of this book. Therefore, I am heartily grateful to all those scholars and learned scholars from whose works I obtained important information to create this book. I also express my gratitude to all those websites from which this book has been written by taking appropriate information and images. I am graetful to my colleagues and friends too for their moral support. I am thankful to my family members too who always stood with me and supported me in many ways. It is hoped that through this book, readers, especially girls and women, will get acquainted with the contribution made by Dr. Ambedkar for women emancipation and empowerment and they will get an opportunity to express their gratitude to women-benefactor Babasaheb Dr. Ambedkar.

Dr. Kuldeep Singh

CHAPTER I

Socio-Political Status of Women: Historical Background

This book attempts to shed light on the vision and contribution of Babasaheb Dr. B.R. Ambedkar as a great feminist and a strong advocate and true warrior for gender equality and women empowerment. As it is a historical fact that across the world, women were confined to the domestic sphere, while public life was reserved for men. Patriarchal and conservative societies across the world denied women the rights to freedom, property, education and participation in public life. That is, women were not given any kind of social, economic and civil rights. Women lived their lives in complete male subordination. They were considered second class citizens compared to men. Only duties were prescribed for women which they had to strictly discharge.

Global Perspective

Not only in India but also in western countries like Europe and America, women had to face inequality, gender discrimination and social injustice. Across the world, women were confined to the domestic sphere, while public life was reserved for men. In medieval Europe, women were denied the right to own property, study or participate in public life. In France in the late 19th century, women were forced to cover their heads in public, and in parts of Germany, a husband had the right to sell his wife. Women had neither social equality nor the political right to vote. To counter this pitiable condition of women, feminist ideas began to take shape, mainly in the Western world.[1]

With regard to women's rights, the situation was also bad in Islamic countries. In these countries, polygamy, which had religious support, was prevalent, due to which women had to face exploitation, harassment and persecution. Undoubtedly, feminist movements in Western countries and India did lead to significant improvement in the condition of women. But, the status quo remained almost the same in the Islamic world. Traditionally, Arab society has also been patriarchal like other societies. As a result, women's access to education, employment opportunities and political participation was often almost negligible. In some conservative communities, women's roles have been primarily confined to the private sphere, focused on family and household responsibilities. Their participation in the public sphere was nil. Most Arab countries, except for countries like Saudi Arabia, started granting political rights to women from the mid-twentieth century. Saudi Arabia gave women the right to vote in 2015.

Indian Perspective

As far as India is concerned, however, the status of women in India was not always so low. From the Vedic period to the present, women have lived a respectable life in the past as well. They have been witness to an empowered life in the past as well. There was no sudden change in the status of women from the post-Vedic period. With the passage of time, numerous restrictions were imposed on women. By the medieval period, the condition of women had become pathetic. Although a positive attitude towards women developed during the Bhakti movement in Indian history, but amid the continuous invasions, women were again imprisoned in their homes. Women were the most exploited in any invasion. Later, the custom of keeping many queens in a harem became common. Women were turned into objects of pleasure.

However, some Indian states were ruled by women even during the British colonial period, including Jhansi (Rani Lakshmibai), Kittur (Rani Chennama), Bhopal (Quidisa Begum) and Punjab (Jind Kaur). But, it is also a bitter truth that women in India experienced a harsher life than other parts of the world in the name of traditions as they were not only deprived of freedom and equality but also did not have the right to life as they were forced to burn themselves along with the dead body of their husband. Widows were not allowed to remarry even if they lost their spouses in childhood.

Girl education was completely prohibited and educating a girl or women was considered a sin i.e. an act against religion. Child marriage and female foeticide were also very heinous social evils prevalent in India. They got no rights except duties. Complete subordination of women was prescribed through religious books. Apart from encouraging caste-based humiliation and exploitation of untouchables and backward castes, the religious books also endorsed the humiliation, exploitation, oppression and subordination of women. This is evident from the following couplet:

Dhol, Ganwar, Shudra, Pashu, Nari.
Ye Sab Tadan Ke Adhikari.

Women were also considered inferior like Shudras. This blocked the path of their progress and they were forced to live a life of subordination and slavery like the backward caste people. They were also deprived of education, property, respect, freedom, equality and justice.

Mata pita bhrata hitkaari, mitprad sab sun rajkumaari
amitdaani bharta baidehi, adham so naari jo sev na tehi

This means the Mother, father, brother are beneficial, benevolent, listen princess, husband is generous, wife is lowly, the woman who does not serve her husband. Through, the above verse of Ramcharitmanas, Maharishi Tulsidas has considered a woman as the servant of her husband and has advised her to serve her husband. He believed that a woman is lowly who does not serve her husband. Lowly means lowly. That is, according to Tulsidas, as he has described in the above verse, a woman who does not serve her husband is lowly. In another verse of Ramcharitmanas, Maharishi Tulsidas has written that

Adham te adham adham ati naari, tin meh me matimand aghari
kah Raghupati sun bhamini baata, manaun ek bhagti ka naata

In the first line above, women have been described as the lowest of the low which is the height of inequality and gender discrimination and humiliation. How can all women be the lowest of the low? This is a serious and thought-provoking question. Such humiliation of women through religious books is extremely painful. This thinking highlights the subordination of women and their exploitation and humiliation. Such a discriminatory system was also reinforced by religious books.

However, Manusmriti in shloka 3.55-3.56, also declares that "women should be respected and adorned", and "where women are respected, the gods are pleased; but where they are not, no sacred ritual bears any fruit". But the Manu Smriti itself declares in verses 5.147-5.148 that "a woman should never try to live independently".[2] It was arranged that women would be subordinate to their fathers in childhood, to their husbands in youth and to their sons in old age. The Manu Smriti established the supremacy of men over women. It was clearly stated that a woman should always worship her husband as God. The condition of women was bad, and if the woman was an untouchable, her condition was even more painful. Untouchable women were not considered Hindus like untouchable men. According to Dr. Ambedkar, the best example of the lack of sensitivity of Hindus towards untouchables is found in the following incident reported by the correspondent of 'Sangram' and published in the issue of 10 July 1946.

The correspondent says:

"On July 8, 1946, a woman died in an orphanage (beggars' home) called Azil, situated in a village called Mapuse (in Goa) and maintained by Christians. It was assumed that the woman was a Hindu. She was alone and had no relations. There was no one to cremate her body. Therefore, to perform the last rites, some Hindus of the village got together. They carried the body out of the beggars' home. About the same time some untouchables came there and recognized the body of the woman. As soon as the Hindus came to know that the dead woman was an untouchable the Hindus who had gathered there fled. The untouchables who had come started to walk away carrying the body and requested the Hindus to give them the money they had collected to buy the coffin and shroud. The Hindus refused, saying that the money was collected on the understanding that the dead woman was a Hindu woman. As she was not a Hindu but an untouchable, they could not spend money on her funeral. The untouchables had to perform the last rites of the woman. This is a good proof of the love and affection of Hindus towards the untouchables."[3]

In fact, upper caste Hindus did not consider untouchables as Hindus and the upper caste people had almost zero sensitivity towards untouchable women. Women had neither freedom nor rights. They were forced to live their lives under complete male domination. Her world was within the four walls of the house and it was forbidden for her to cross the threshold in the absence of a man. Some old men started raising their voices to get women out of this pitiable condition. Only then did the change in the social, educational, economic and political status of women come which we can see today. A great credit for this change goes to Babasaheb Dr. Bhimrao Ramji Ambedkar who made concrete provisions for women empowerment during the British rule and as the architect of the Constitution. This contribution of his has been highlighted in the following chapters.

Rise of Feminism and Feminist Thinkers

As it is well known that in ancient and medieval times, women were given equal rights and were not given equal rights. Not only were the social, economic and political conditions extremely bad but even in the modern times, all over the world, they had to face exploitation, oppression and harassment. In countries like France, women were forced to cover their heads in public places, and in some parts of Germany, a husband even had the right to sell his wife. Clearly, the wife was treated as a commodity. Women had neither social equality nor political rights like voting. To counter this pitiable condition of women, feminist ideas began to take shape mainly in the western world. However, there are rare examples of feminist thought mainly in the ancient world.

In a simple sense, the ideology of women's rights and social equality is called feminism, which opposes gender inequality and discrimination and strongly demands equal rights for women by considering them equal to men. Feminism is a category of social and political movements and ideologies, which share a goal of defining, establishing and achieving gender equality politically, economically, personally and socially. Famous feminist thinker poet Golendra Patel has said in the context of feminism that "Women's discourse from a woman's perspective is that human thought stream which awakens women's consciousness and advocates their freedom, this is called feminism in women's language.[4]

Feminism believes that society gives priority to male perspective and in these patriarchal societies, women are discriminated and treated unjustly.[5] Simone de Beauvoir says, "Woman is not born, she is made." Society has been molding women according to its needs. From her thinking to her way of living, men have controlled her till date and continue to try to do so even today. The patriarchal society has decided everything according to its own will.[6]

Feminist Thinkers in the Middle Ages

The defense of women had become a literary subgenre by the end of the 16th century, when Il merito delle donne (1600; The Worth of Woman), a feminist book written by another Venetian author, Moderata Fonte, was published posthumously. Defenders of the status quo depicted women as superficial and inherently immoral, while emerging feminists compiled long lists of women of courage and achievement and declared that if women were given equal access to education, they would be the intellectual equals of men.[7]

As far as medieval and modern times are concerned, Mary Wollstonecraft was the primary feminist who initiated the discussion on women's issues and raised her voice for gender equality and women's empowerment in her 'A Vindication of the Rights of Woman: With Strictures on Political and Moral Subjects'. 1792. After the Enlightenment, women began demanding reforms such as freedom, equality, and natural rights that applied to both sexes. Initially, Enlightenment philosophers shifted focus from the exclusion of gender to the inequalities of social class and caste. For example, Swiss-born French philosopher Jean-Jacques

Rousseau depicted women as stupid and trivial creatures who were born to be subservient to men. Furthermore, the Declaration of the Rights of Man and of the Citizen, which defined French citizenship after the Revolution of 1789, failed blatantly to address women's legal status.

Female intellectuals of the Enlightenment were quick to point out the lack of inclusiveness and limited scope of reformist rhetoric. Olympe de Gouges, a famous playwright, published the Déclaration des droits de la femme et de la citoyenne (1791; "Declaration of the Rights of Woman and of the Citizen"), declaring woman not only to be man's equal but his partner. The following year Mary Wollstonecraft's A Vindication of the Rights of Woman (1792), the seminal feminist work in the English language, was published in England. Challenging the notion that women exist only to please men, she proposed that women and men be given equal opportunities in education, work, and politics. Women are naturally as rational as men, she wrote. If they are stupid, it is only because society trains them to be irrelevant.[8]

J.S. Mill was another great feminist who wrote the world-famous work Subjection of Women to highlight the pitiable plight of women and raised a vibrant voice in favour of women along with his wife Harriet Taylor. Subjection of Women was published in 1869. In this essay, Mill argues in favour of legal and social equality between men and women. He writes that 'the "legal subjection" of one sex to the other is wrong in itself, and one of the chief obstacles to human improvement. It was widely believed that women were more emotional than rational, and lacked intellectual abilities. But Mill rejected this belief prevalent in his time. Mill argues that if women seem emotional, passive, and apolitical, it is because they have been raised to be that way. In making this claim, Mill reiterates Mary Wollstonecraft's Vindication of the Rights of Woman.

Mill emphasises that unless society treats men and women equally, it will be impossible to know the natural capacities of women. The question that arises here is whether there are inherent differences between the sexes. The obvious answer is that there is only physical difference between men and women. Apart from this, there is no difference between women and men, neither in intelligence, nor in reasoning power, nor in understanding. What is meant to say is that women are not inferior in any way. If women are given proper education or better training, then women will not prove to be inferior to men in any matter. Just as all men are not mentally and physically strong, similarly some women may also not be so, but such women can be made mentally and physically strong by training. The persons, texts or sects which declare women to be mentally and physically weak are indeed corrupt and inhuman. Like Wollstonecraft and Margaret Fuller (1810-1913), Mill articulated and defended the rights of women, rather than making them dependent on what society thinks they should do or be. Mill was confident that women, even if given freedom and opportunities, would not fail to perform their traditional functions. Mill believed that women were as bright and talented as men, and once given the same eagerness for fame, women would achieve the same. Through his The Subject, Mill made a strong claim for equal status in three major areas which were as follows – right to vote for women, right to equal opportunity in education and employment.[9]

In short, Mill sincerely advocated the social, economic and political upliftment of women. Though the efforts of feminist movements led to the improvement in the social and economic status of women, political empowerment could not come to them so easily. Even in Europe, women were completely denied political rights, mainly the right to vote. Europe and America, considered advanced countries and mature democracies, did not grant women the right to vote for a long time. Even in post-revolution France, the issue of granting political rights to women was a controversial issue within the liberal movement, in which a large number of women had actively participated over the years. Women formed their own political associations, founded newspapers and participated in political meetings and demonstrations. Despite this, they were denied the right to vote during assembly elections. When the Frankfurt Parliament convened in St. Paul's Church, women stood in the gallery only as observers.[10] Women had to struggle hard for voting rights. Ultimately, as a result of feminist movements and struggle, women in most countries of the world got social and economic as well as political rights. The struggle for women's rights in India is depicted through the next chapter.

References

1. https://www.britannica.com/topic/feminism

2. Patrick Olivelle (2005), Manu's Code of Law, Oxford University Press, ISBN 978-0195171464, p. 111

3. DR AMBEDKAR WRITINGS Volume_4

4. "Feminism | Definition, History, Types, Waves, Examples, & Facts | Britannica" also wikipedia

5. Gamble, Sarah (2001). "The Routledge Companion to Feminism and Postfeminism also wikipedia

6. श्रुति गौतम (वी आई पी एस) दिल्ली):

https://www.drishtiias.com/hindi/blog/womenempowerment-inindia#:~:text=%E0%A4%A1%E0%A5%89.,%E0%A4%B8%E0%A4%AE%E0%A4%BE%E0%A4%9C%20%E0%A4%95%E0%A5%80%20%E0%A4%86%E0%A4%A7%E0%A5%80%20%E0%A4%86%E0%A4%AC%E0%A4%BE%E0%A4%A6%E0%A5%80%20%E0%A4%B9%E0%A5%88%E0%A4%82%E0%A5%A4

7. https://www.britannica.com/topic/feminism

8. https://www.britannica.com/topic/feminism

9. Mukherjee, S. and Ramaswamy, S. (2003): *A History of Political Thought-Plato to Marx,* Prentice Hall of India Private Limited, New Delhi.

10. NCERT Book for 10th class (2006): *India and the Contemporary World II.*

CHAPTER II

Women Emancipation and Empowerment in India: Ideological Ground

Although, in Europe, J.S. Mill had made a strong case for equal status and equal opportunity for women in three major areas- right to vote, right to education and equal opportunity in employment. But, the foundation of women's movement in the world was laid only in the 19th century. Many nations of the West became participants in this movement during that period. It was only when the women's movement came to the fore that the concept of women empowerment came to the fore prominently. Therefore, to understand women empowerment, it is also very important to understand the women's movement. In simple words, the women's movement started against the disgusting thinking of the society which considers women inferior, which considers women to be inferior to men and establishes the supremacy of men over women. The important principle of feminism is that women have an inferior status in this patriarchal society. This patriarchal society itself constitutes the rules and form of living for her. It denies the independent personality of women. The women's movement does not oppose any man but the patriarchal idea. This movement believes that women should get equal respect, rights and opportunities as men. Nari Andolan is in favour of gender equality instead of gender inequality and believes in the concept that women are also human beings and being a human being, they are also entitled to all the rights that men should get.

Women Movements and Women Empowerment

To understand women empowerment, it is also very important to understand Nari Andolan. Feminism is an idea and movement that rejects gender inequality and emphasizes on equality between men and women. It advocates giving women all those rights and freedoms that men get as humans. In simple words, Nari Andolan started when society considered women to be inferior. An important principle of feminism is that in this patriarchal society, women have an inferior status. This society itself forms the rules and form of living for them. It rejects the independent personality of women. Nari Andolan does not oppose any man but the patriarchal idea. This movement believes that women should also get equal respect, rights and opportunities as men. The women's movement believes in the concept that women are also human beings instead of gender inequality. Along with being human, they are half the population of the world. They have as much contribution in the creation of the world as men.[1]

In this chapter, an attempt has been made to understand the ideological basis of women's empowerment in India and an attempt has been made to underline the contribution of other social reformers and thinkers who raised their voice for women's interests besides Babasaheb Dr. Ambedkar. Also, the background of the struggle for gender justice and equality in India has been mentioned. Among Indian social reformers and thinkers, Raja Ram Mohan Roy, Keshav Chandra Vidyasagar, Jyotirao Phule and his wife Savitribai Phule can be considered as the early feminists in India. Jyotirao Phule and Savitribai Phule were the pioneers of women's education in India. Phule started his first school for girls in Pune in 1848. He also formed the Satyashodhak Samaj. Raja Ram Mohan Roy, Keshav Chandra Vidyasagar etc. have addressed many social and religious evils including women's issues.

Raja Ram Mohan Roy' Contribution

Raja Ram Mohan Roy founded the Atmiya Sabha and the Unitarian community to fight social evils and propagate social and educational reforms in India. He was a fighter against superstitions, a pioneer of Indian education and a trend setter in Bengali prose and the Indian press. He campaigned against Hindu practices like sati, polygamy, child marriage and the caste system. He demanded the right of inheritance of property for women. In 1828, he founded the Brahmo Sabha, a movement of reformist Bengali Brahmins to fight against social evils. Ram Mohan Roy was against the practice of sati and strongly criticized it. With his genuine efforts, Lord William Bentinck banned the practice of sati in 1829, in which a widowed woman had to burn herself along with the dead body of her husband. Truly, it was a heinous and cruel act that was going on in the name of religion and tradition.[2]

Ishwarchandra Vidyasagar's Role

Ishwarchandra Vidyasagar understood the importance of education and firmly believed that the upliftment of India was possible only through education. He also laid special emphasis on women's education. He also wrote books and articles on various subjects like history, literature and science to promote the intellectual development of women. He believed that education was the key to empowering women and enabling them to fully participate in society. Ishwarchandra spent his early life in the village as a result of which he realized the pitiable and sad condition of women. He believed that as long as women remained ignorant, their liberation was not possible. Therefore, Ishwarchandra took upon himself the task of promoting women's education. Seeing the indifference of the British government towards women's education, Ishwarchandra himself started some model schools for girls. He also collaborated with Drinkwater Bethune in establishing the Hindu Women's School (present Bethune School and College of Kolkata) in 1849.[3]

Ishwarchandra Vidyasagar was opposed to those traditions of Hindu society which made the life of women hell. One of those traditions was the prohibition of widow remarriage. That is, a woman was not allowed to remarry after her husband died. The widowed woman or girl had to live the rest of her life as a widow even if the girl became a widow at a young age. In fact, this was an inhuman tradition which was a big problem for women's interests. She advocated legalizing widow remarriage, which was forbidden at that time. Despite facing strong opposition from conservative groups, she filed a petition in the Legislative Council to allow widows to remarry. She also encouraged her son to marry a widow. Her efforts led to the passing of the Hindu Widow Remarriage Act of 1856, which gave widows the right to remarry and own property. She campaigned against the practice of polygamy, which was prevalent among upper caste Hindu men. She argued that polygamy is unjust and immoral and it violates the dignity and rights of women. He also highlighted social and economic problems such as domestic violence, poverty and child neglect caused by polygamy. He supported the Civil Marriage Act of 1872, which banned polygamy and child marriage. Ishwar Chandra Vidyasagar was a visionary leader who dedicated his life to women empowerment and social reform. He was a man of many facets and a source of knowledge.[4] He also advocated the recognition of human rights for all. He was a pioneer of social justice and humanism in India. He is considered one of the key figures of India's renaissance in the nineteenth century.

Jyotirao Govindrao Phule and his wife Savitribai Phule: Their Efforts towards Women's Education and Empowerment

Jyotirao Govindrao Phule (11 April 1827 – 28 November 1890) and his wife Savitribai Phule are considered worthy feminists in India. He was an Indian social activist, thinker, anti-caste social reformer and writer from Maharashtra. His work spanned many areas, including the eradication of untouchability and the caste system and his efforts to educate women and lower caste people. He and his wife, Savitribai Phule, were pioneers of women's education in India. Phule started his first school for girls in 1848 at Tatyasaheb Bhide's residence or Bhidewada in Pune. He, along with his followers, formed the Satyashodhak Samaj (Society of Truth Seekers) to achieve equal rights for lower caste people (Wikipedia). He was an iconic and unique activist and reformer who not only supported and encouraged women's upliftment, but he also encouraged his wife, Savitribai Phule, to read, write, and dream of a society where women did not have to depend on men. He supported widow remarriage and in 1863 started a home for pregnant widows of upper castes to give birth in a safe place. His orphanage was founded in an effort to reduce the rate of infanticide. On 24 September 1873, Phule formed the Satyashodhak Samaj to focus on the rights of oppressed groups such as women, Shudras and Dalits.[5]

Jyotiba's ideas and efforts to provide women and girls the right to education were supported by his wife Savitribai Phule. Savitribai, one of the few literate women of that time, was taught to read and write at home by her husband Jyotirao. In 1851, Jyotiba founded a girls' school and asked his wife to teach the girls at the school. Later, they opened two more schools for girls and an indigenous school for the lower castes, especially the Mahars and Mangs. Jyotiba realized the pitiable conditions of widows and founded an ashram for young widows and eventually became a supporter of the idea of widow remarriage. Around his time, the society was a patriarchal one and the condition of women was particularly poor. Female foeticide was a common phenomenon and there was also child marriage, sometimes marrying children to much older men. These women often became widows before attaining puberty and were left without any family support. Jyotiba was pained by their plight and in 1854 he founded an orphanage to save these unfortunate souls from perishing at the cruel hands of society.[6]

Jyotiba Phule was undoubtedly the great pioneer of equality, social justice and women empowerment of the 19th century. He used the weapon of education to attack the prevailing ignorance, superstition and hypocrisy in the society and also took revolutionary and historic steps towards equality, social justice and women empowerment. Jyotiba waged a remarkable struggle against social evils, especially untouchability and caste discrimination and social injustice through the Satyashodhak Samaj. By writing the book Gulamgiri, he strongly attacked caste-based discrimination, exploitation, oppression and injustice and raised a strong voice for the rights of Dalits, backward classes and women. Undoubtedly,

Jyotiba Phule laid the foundation of the struggle for social justice in modern India, which proved to be a source of inspiration for Dr. Ambedkar and other pioneers of social justice. Dr. Ambedkar not only took inspiration from Mahatma Jyotiba Phule, but also considered him as his political guru and achieved unprecedented success in taking the struggle for social justice to new heights. Jyotiba Phule's ideology and his contribution in the fight for equality and social justice will also serve as a guide for the coming generations.

Contribution of Savitribai Phule for Girl Education and Upliftment of Women

Savitribai Phule made a significant contribution in the education of girls and the upliftment of women. It was her passion for girls‘ education that led her, along with her husband Jyotiba Phule, to build and open the first school for girls. Savitribai Phule believed that education is very important for the progress of women. She used to say that 'education is the real jewel of women‘. Savitribai is also remembered for fighting for the rights of widows, campaigning for the abolition of child marriage, founding the 'Home for the Prevention of Infanticide and the Protection of Pregnant Women‘ in 1863, and for being a prolific poetess. Her poetry mainly dealt with issues of education, caste, and nature. After completing her education to become a teacher, Savitribai Phule began teaching girls in Maharwada, Pune. She did so with Sagunabai who was a revolutionary feminist as well as a mentor to Jyotirao.

Shortly after she began teaching with Sagunabai, Savitribai and Jyotirao Phule joined Sagunabai to start their own school in Bhidewada. Bhidewada was the home of Tatya Saheb Bhide, who was inspired by the work the three were doing. The curriculum at Bhidewada included traditional Western curriculum in mathematics, science, and social studies. By the end of 1851, Savitribai and Jyotirao Phule were running three separate schools for girls in Pune. Combined, the three schools had about one hundred and fifty students enrolled. Like the curriculum, the teaching methods employed by the three schools were different from those used in government schools. Author, Divya Kandukuri believes that the Phule methods were considered superior to those used by government schools. As a result of this reputation, the number of girls receiving their education in Phule's schools was higher than the number of boys enrolled in government schools.[7]

Unfortunately, Savitribai and Jyotirao Phule's success came with much resistance from the local community with a conservative mindset.

Kandukuri states that Savitribai often travelled to her school carrying an extra sari because she was harassed by her conservative opponents with stones, cow dung and verbal abuse. The Phule's faced such strong opposition because of the orthodox (Brahmin) and marginalized caste to which they belonged. The Sudra community had been deprived of education for thousands of years. For this reason, many Brahmins opposed the work of Jyotirao and Savitribai and labelled it as 'evil'. By 1849, Savitribai and Jyotirao Phule were living at Jyotirao's father's house. However, in 1849, Jyotirao's father asked the couple to leave his house because their work was considered a sin according to Brahminical texts.[8] After being thrown out of their own father's house, the Phule couple moved in with the family of Usman Sheikh, a friend of Jyotirao. There, Savitribai soon became a close friend and associate of Fatima Begum Sheikh. According to Nasreen Sayyed, a leading scholar, "Fatima Sheikh already knew how to read and write, her brother Usman who was Jyotiba's friend, encouraged Fatima to start a teacher training course. She went to the normal school with Savitribai and both graduated together.[9]

Fatima Sheikh and Women Education

Fatima Sheikh was also a great feminist and teacher, who was an associate of social reformers Jyotiba Phule and Savitribai Phule. Fatima Sheikh was the sister of Mian Usman Sheikh, in whose house Jyotiba and Savitribai Phule stayed. One of the first Muslim women teachers of modern India, she began educating Dalit children in Phule's school. Jyotiba and Savitribai Phule, along with Fatima Sheikh, took up the task of spreading education among Dalit communities. Savitribai and Jyotirao Phule had to leave their home because they wanted to educate women and Dalits. The starting of these schools was met with sharp and even violent reactions from the upper caste people. When Fatima and Savitribai were on their way, they threw stones and cow dung at them. But the two women remained undeterred. As stated in many accounts, Fatima would spend hours counselling parents who did not want to send their girls to school.[10]

Pandit Ramabai's Struggle for Women's Emancipation

During the nineteenth century, when the cause of women was being taken up by social reformers during many reform movements in India and when most women's reform movements were dominated by men, Pandita Ramabai (1858-1922) was a uniquely distinguished female social reformer of the time, as she led early feminism in India and fought throughout her life for the emancipation of Indian women. With her exceptional scholarly background, she became a pillar of women's educational rights and social reform in Indian society. Pandita Ramabai is one of the few early voices of women in colonial India. Her aim was to ensure self-reliance for women. To empower women she attempted to create women reform consciousness. Through her writings in Marathi and English, she has always raised issues related to women's education and self-reliance. Pandita Ramabai was known for her activities towards women's emancipation, freedom and education.

Pandita's actual reform career began with the establishment of the first organisation for women in Maharashtra, Arya Mahila Samaj (Arya Women's Society) in Poona on 1 June 1882, which aimed to lead the emancipation of women, discuss and change certain practices such as child marriage, cruel treatment of widows, etc. By the end of June 1882 she published her first book (in Marathi) 'Stri Dharma Niti' (Morality for Women). The book sold very well and it is believed that she wrote and published this work to earn some money; possibly she used this money to pay for the expenses of her trip to England the following year.

She wanted to address women-related issues more seriously, which many social reformers of her time failed to take forward. Being a widow herself and knowing the condition of widows and helpless women of upper castes, Ramabai thought of taking up their cause. By this time Ramabai realised the place of modern education and how she could advance because of it. She was not willing to miss any opportunity that could be helpful for women. In the year 1882, the Government of India had appointed a commission (The Hunter Education Commission) which was to oversee education in India and Ramabai gave evidence before the commission and suggested that teachers should be trained for their jobs and more women should be appointed.

She argued strongly for the need for general as well as medical education for women. She insisted on the appointment of female teachers and doctors to educate and treat girls and pointed out that women would have great difficulty in explaining their problems to male teachers or doctors. Impressed by her views and ability to communicate, Sir Hunter, the chairman of the commission, translated her views from Marathi into English and publicised her suggestions for women's medical education and the need for women doctors, which greatly influenced the thinking of Queen Victoria. According to Dr. Kosambi, the dissemination of Ramabai's testimony and Dr. Hunter's personal activity on the subject may have inspired the creation of the Dufferin Fund to provide medical aid to Indian women.''[11]

Mahatma Gandhi's Views reagarding Women Emancipation

Mahatma Gandhi also raised his voice for women. Gandhiji also participated in the national freedom movement. However, Gandhiji believed that it is the duty of women to look after home and hearth, to be a good mother and a good wife. And for a long time the Congress was reluctant to keep women in any prominent position in the organisation.[12] However, Gandhiji also believed that women have the same mental capacities as men and hence they should have equal rights. However, due to custom, ignorant and worthless men are enjoying superiority over women. (Speeches and Writings of Mahatma Gandhi) Gandhi criticised the Manusmriti for its humiliation of women.[13]

Gandhi was totally opposed to gender discrimination. Gandhi did not like the preference for boys in Indian society and the general neglect of the girl child. In fact, in most cases she (the girl child) is not allowed to be born. If she is born, her survival is not assured. If she somehow survives, she is neglected. She does not get the same respect and status as a boy which she deserves. As already stated, he termed discrimination against women as anachronistic: He said: "I see no reason to rejoice at the birth of a son and to mourn at the birth of a daughter. Both are gifts of God. They have equal rights. They are equally necessary to live and to keep the world going." Gandhi called women the noblest sex. He said that if she is weak to strike, she is strong to suffer. Gandhi described; "Woman is the epitome of sacrifice and non-violence." He further adds: "The daughter's share should be equal to that of the son. The husband's earnings are the joint property of the husband and wife because he earns money with her help."[14]

Periyar's Support for Women's RightsPeriyar was a great supporter of women's rights. Periyar was an egalitarian thinker and agitator and was strongly opposed to caste as well as gender inequality. Being an egalitarian, he was inclined towards Buddhism because Buddhism not only is based on equality but also strongly promotes it. Hence, from 1927, E.V. Ramaswami became interested in propagating the principles of Buddhism and highlighting the teachings of Thirukkural. Being an egalitarian, he was also critical of gender inequality and was a major advocate of women's rights and empowerment. He was also a strong advocate of women's education and championed women's interests for equal rights.

Dr. Ram Manohar Lohia: An Advocate of War against Caste and Gender Segregation

Dr. Lohia laid main emphasis on caste and gender segregation rather than class segregation. He believed that caste and gender discrimination had led to an unjust social, economic and cultural system in India. In his work The Two Segregations of Caste and Sex, Lohia said, "All war against poverty is a sham, unless it is, at the same time, a conscious and sustained war on these two segregations". Lohia considered caste and sex segregation to be the main responsible factors for injustice against Dalits, backward classes and women. Therefore, he wanted to launch a war against these two segregations of caste and sex. He wanted to create a society free from inequality and discrimination based on the two segregations of caste and sex in which women have an empowered position and there is no gender discrimination of any kind. Thus, Lohia was a notable supporter of women's rights and their empowerment.

Undoubtedly, the true seeds of women's empowerment in India were sown by Mahatma Jyotiba Phule and his life partner Savitribai Phule. Though Ram Mohan Roy and Ishwar Chandra Vidyasagar had started raising their voice for women's interests, their main focus was on the abolition of Sati and widow remarriage. Important work for women's education and women's rights was done by warriors of social justice like Jyotiba Phule, Savitribai Phule, Fatima Sheikh, E.V. Ramasamy (Periyar), Dr. Bhimrao Ambedkar, Dr. Ram Manohar Lohia. Along with this, it would not be an exaggeration to say that the most wonderful and remarkable role for women's empowerment and women's rights was played by Babasaheb Dr. Ambedkar, due to which Babasaheb is called the destiny maker of Dalits as well as the liberator of women. In the next chapters of this book, the contribution of Dr. Ambedkar in women's empowerment has been highlighted.

Reference

1. श्रुति गौतम (वी आई पी एस) दिल्ली):

https://www.drishtiias.com/hindi/blog/women-empowerment-in
india#:~:text=%E0%A4%A1%E0%A5%89.,%E0%A4%B8%E0%A4%A
E%E0%A4%BE%E0%A4%9C%20%E0%A4%95%E0%A5%80%20%E0%A
4%86%E0%A4%A7%E0%A5%80%20%E0%A4%86%E0%A4%AC%E0%A
4%BE%E0%A4%A6%E0%A5%80%20%E0%A4%B9%E0%A5%88%E0%
A4%82%E0%A5%A4)

2. https://en.wikipedia.org/wiki/Ram_Mohan_Roy#Social_reforms

3. preservearticles.com

4. keshawchandra vidya sagar's contribution for wpmen empowerment -Search (bing.com)

5. https://en.wikipedia.org/wiki/Jyotiao_Phule#Women's_welfare

6. https://feminisminindia.com/2017/04/14/jotiba-phule-gulamgiri/

7. Kandukuri, Divya (11 January 2019). "The life and times of Savitribai Phule", Mint.

8. Kandukuri, Divya (11 January 2019). "The life and times of Savitribai Phule", Mint.

9. https://www.deccanherald.com/content/651578/savitribai-phule-women-rights-champion.html

10. https://en.wikipedia.org/wiki/Fatima_Sheikh

11. https://www.questjournals.org/jrhss/papers/vol10-issue9/1009151154.pdf

12. class-10-NCERT BOOK Social Science-India and the Contemporary World-II (Chapter-2)

13. www.sacredtext.com

14. https://www.mkgandhi.org/articles/womenempowerment.
htm#:~:text=Gandhiji%20called%20women%
20as%20the,to%20that%20of%20a%20son.

CHAPTER III

Dr. Ambedkar as a Great Feminist Thinker: His Vission For Women Empowerment

After discussing other feminist thinkers in the previous chapter, an attempt has been made in this chapter to present Babasaheb Dr. B.R. Ambedkar as a strong feminist thinker and a strong fighter for the dignity of women and depressed people as well. In fact, Dr. Ambedkar had a great vision as far as women empowerment was concerned. He believed in the complete emancipation and empowerment of women and gave concrete shape to the ideological foundation laid by Jyotiba Phule, Savitribai Phule, Fatima Sheikh, etc. for women empowerment. He gave a new edge to feminist thinking and paved a solid path for women empowerment. Therefore, from this chapter onwards, an attempt has been made to highlight the special role of Dr. Ambedkar in the field of women empowerment.

Supporter of Adequate Participation of Women

Dr. Ambedkar was the first Indian to break the barriers in the way of advancement of women in India.He was a great ideological supporter of women's adequate participation in all spheres of life. He did not want women to be confined only to domestic affairs. Babasaheb strongly believed in the abilities and capabilities of women and was in favour of enhancing their capabilities by involving them in public affairs.He laid the foundation of concrete and honest efforts by codifying the same code for Hindus and other sections of Indian society. He said that women should be given all-round development and more important social education, their well-being and socio-cultural rights. He emphasized that every class of Indian women should be given their fair share and that it is important to maintain and protect the dignity and modesty of women.[1]

Strongly advocated women's issues

Dr. Ambedkar was a strong advocate of equality and social justice. As a supporter of social justice, he believed social justice was incomplete without gender equality and women empowerment. He also included women in the fight for equality and social justice. Dr. Ambedkar strongly advocated women's issues and raised them on several fronts wherever he got the opportunity. Dr. Ambedkar also strongly raised women's issues in the

Bombay Legislative Assembly on 10 November 1938. During this time, he also expressed his views on concerns related to childbirth.

Prominent advocate of women's rights

Dr. Ambedkar was a prominent advocate of women's rights. From his student days, he was a strong advocate of making women capable and self-reliant in every aspect. Women's empowerment was always an important part of his thinking, which is enough to prove him to be a serious feminist thinker and a sharp speaker. Ambedkar's views on the question of women, his emphasis on the right to education, equal treatment with men, right to property and participation in the political process were similar to the demands of global feminists. As expressed by J.S. Mill in his book Subjection of Women, legal subordination of one sex to the other is wrong in itself and one of the main obstacles to human development; and it should be replaced by the principle of complete equality, in which there should be no privilege or power on one side, nor disability on the other. Ambedkar also held equal views on work for women.[2]

An amazing advocate of gender equality

Dr. Ambedkar was an amazing advocate of gender equality and was a strong critic of the dominance of men over women. He understood gender equality since his student days. There is no doubt that Dr. Ambedkar considered women equal to men and was a strong supporter of providing them equal rights in every respect. When he got the opportunity to write the Constitution of India, he implemented his thoughts and gave all the fundamental, legal, economic and political rights to women. Adopting the principle of one man one vote one value, he provided universal suffrage and gave equal opportunity to women to become politically influential like men.

Awareness among uneducated women

Dr. Ambedkar created awareness among poor uneducated women and inspired them to fight against unjust and social practices like child marriage and Devdasi system. Dr. Babasaheb Ambedkar said, I strongly believe in the movements being run by women. If they are really taken into confidence, they can change the present picture of the society which is very pathetic. In the past, they have played an important role in improving the condition of weaker sections and classes. He always respected work and hardships. While addressing women in conferences, he used to communicate and talk with them easily like a household person. Dr. Babasaheb spent his life for the betterment of women. According to Dr. Ambedkar, society should be based on reason and not on the cruel traditions of the caste system.

Therefore, in The Annihilation of Caste, he has given the key suggestion for the elimination of caste created through scriptures, "Free every man and woman from the slavery of scriptures and purify their minds of the harmful notions based on scriptures and they will make a difference. People of all castes should eat together and intermarry".

Belief in women-led movements

Dr. Babasaheb Ambedkar always supported women participation in movements and he believed in women-led movements too. He also said that if women from all walks of life are taken into confidence, they can play an important role in social reforms. They have played a very big and active role in eliminating social abuses. He emphasized that every married woman should participate in the activities of her husband as a friend. But she must show the courage to refuse the life of slaves. She must emphasize the principle of equality. If all women follow this, they will get real respect and their identity.[3] In other words, it can be said that Babasaheb Dr. Ambedkar was not only a supporter of women's participation in public life but he also wanted to create leadership power in women, for which he also inspired women to lead movements. It is clear that Dr. Ambedkar was a master of very advanced and progressive thoughts and was strongly opposed to considering women as second class citizens in any way.

His Effort to instill self-respect in women

In 1942 itself, in the meeting of All India Dalit Women's Federation, Dr. Ambedkar appealed to Dalit women not to marry their daughters at an early age, and stressed on educating them and standing on their own feet. While giving the message of having fewer children and living cleanly, he also talked about women having a level of equality in families. While instilling self-respect in women, he said that you should live in an equal relationship in the house by becoming a friend of the husband and not as a slave of the husband. After the establishment of Scheduled Caste Federation in Nagpur in 1942, Shanta Bai Dani was made the District President of the party in the Scheduled Caste Federation meeting in Nasik. In 1944, in the second session of Dalit Federation in Kanpur, women held their own independent session and resolutions similar to Nagpur were passed. It was presided over by Miss Shanta Bai Dani. Baba Saheb participated in this session and said, "You move forward, a golden dawn has entered your life."[4]

Advocate of women's participation in decision making process

In the meetings of All India Dalit Women's Federation, Dr. Ambedkar encouraged Dalit women to participate in the decision making process regarding the marriage of their daughters and the matters of having children by themselves. He stressed on women not only educating their girls but also standing on their own feet. He openly supported the equality of women in families. He instilled self-respect in women and encouraged them to become self-reliant. Along with this, it was believed that husband and wife are complementary to each other. Therefore, they should live as friends and live in a relationship of equality and not with feelings of being superior or inferior. We can say that Babasaheb Dr. Ambedkar was never in favour of keeping the status of women in the family low in any way, therefore he wanted women's participation in family decisions. He was also an advocate of full participation of women in public life and administration, therefore he strongly advocated for giving all kinds of rights to women.

Reference

1. Shukla, D. (2011) Dr. BR Ambedkar's Vision towards Gender Equality, Retrieved from http://www.lawyersclubinindia.com

2. More, Vijay G (2011), Dr B.R. Ambedkar's Contribution for Women Rights, Variorum, Multi-Disciplinary e-Research Journal, Vol. 2, Issue-I

3. Gunjal, VR (2012). Dr. Babasaheb Ambedkar and Women Emporment, Social Work, Vol.XI(1), PP 84

4. https://velivada.com/2017/09/03/dr-ambedkar-main-philosophy-women-empowerment/

CHAPTER IV

Dr. Ambedkar: A Great Advocate of Women's Education

Babasaheb Dr. Ambedkar, besides being a renowned jurist, economist and constitutional expert, was a highly educated person, professor, educationist and a leading global thinker. His personality had many facets. This chapter sheds light on Babasaheb's thoughts and efforts regarding education, especially women's education. Dr. Ambedkar gave great importance to education in his life and he emphasized that only through education can man prosper. Babasaheb Ambedkar believed that education is the birthright of every person and no one can be deprived of this right. Babasaheb Dr. Ambedkar was a victim of social discrimination since his childhood and he had to struggle a lot for his education. The contractors of religion were strongly opposed to the education of the exploited, deprived, backward and women and considered their education against religion and a sin. Dr. Ambedkar believed that education was everyone's right and was a great advocate of education of the underprivileged and backward as well as women. However, before Babasaheb, Mahatma Jyotiba Phule and his life partner Savitribai Phule had started educating the underprivileged and girls by encouraging their education. They had laid special emphasis on girl education due to which they had to face a lot of problems.

Special love for education and an advocate of women education

Babasaheb Dr. Ambedkar had a special love for education. He was highly educated and the 'most educated person' of his time. Although, he had to face a lot of hurdles and struggles in his studies, yet he never gave up the idea of studying and continued his studies. Due to untouchability, he had to sit away from other students and also had to remain thirsty in school. He has written in his autobiography, '**no peon, no water**.' This means that on the day the peon did not come to school, the child Ambedkar had to remain thirsty because he did not have the right to touch the utensils. But Babasaheb did not lose courage and he continued to gain education. Babasaheb received education from London, India, America and received many higher degrees. Dr. Ambedkar was very fond of reading, he used to study for eighteen hours every day. He used to get so busy in studying that he used to stay awake till late at night. When people asked him why he studied till so late at night, his answer was that I stay awake till late at night because my society is sleeping. Actually, the purpose of Babasaheb to study till late night was to break the shackles of slavery of the exploited, deprived society and women. He had earned four PhD degrees including postgraduate degrees in many subjects. He knew eight languages. Despite this, his thirst for knowledge did not quench and he remained continuously busy in studies.

His knowledge acquisition had only one goal and that was to build a better India for the exploited, deprived classes and women. Babasaheb Ambedkar has also worked as a professor. His educational qualification, scholarship and talent are so wide and brilliant that he is known as the 'world's most intelligent person' as well as the 'symbol of knowledge'. Babasaheb kept striving for the education of all Indians along with untouchables and women. On 2 May 1954 in Mahad, he advised that "Students should go from slum to slum and remove the ignorance and foolish beliefs of the people, only then their education will benefit the people. Using our knowledge only to pass the examination will not be enough. We should use our knowledge to improve and progress our brothers and sisters; only then India will prosper". Education is the medium of social change. Stay hungry when the time comes but educate your children. He used to say, "If you have two rupees, then take bread worth one rupee and a book worth one rupee. Because bread will help you to live and the book will teach you to live".[1]

Dr. Ambedkar had a special love for books. He used to spend most of his time with books. He said, "I like the company of books more than the company of people". He also said that I want to live my whole life as a student. His personal library had several thousand books. At the time of his death, his personal library is said to have 35000 books. The number of books shows that his personal library was the largest private library in the world and probably even today there is no such private library in which such a large number of books are available.

Rajgir (now Rajgir) is a popular place for Ambedkarite Buddhists and Dalits. Dr. Ambedkar lived in Rajgir for 15-20 years. Ambedkar collected more than 50,000 books during his tenure in Rajgir, making it one of the largest private libraries in the world at the time of his death.[2] The building became a heritage monument in 2013.[3] Thus, undoubtedly Dr. Ambedkar was a great book lover and thirsty for knowledge. Seeing his vast knowledge,

Columbia University of America gave him the title of 'Symbol of Knowledge'. Without the education of Dalits and women, the development of the country is a daydream. Babasaheb Dr. Ambedkar considered education to be the backbone of the development of any country. He used to say that, "Talking about the development of the country without the education of Dalits and women is like daydreaming", so he laid special emphasis on women's education along with Dalits and said that women should also be given the right to freedom and equality. Women should be given equal education as men so that they can contribute to the development of the country by standing shoulder to shoulder with men. Babasaheb says that today's girls will play various roles in the society tomorrow like mother-in-law, daughter-in-law, mother etc., so if they are educated and cultured then the society will develop automatically. If the women of the entire country are educated, then the country will also be on the path of development and the country will definitely be able to regain its lost reputation of Vishwa Guru once again.

Education is a medium to bring equality

Various scholars have expressed their views on the meaning and importance of education, in which the main thing is that education teaches humility and makes a person capable. Whereas Baba Saheb Dr. Ambedkar, apart from all this, has described education not only as a medium to develop social harmony and human qualities, but has also described education as a medium to bring equality in the society. Explaining the meaning of education, he said that the best education is that which not only makes a person literate but also awakens his self-respect and conscience while developing his mentality. In the words of Baba Saheb – "Only education can bring equality in the society." When a person becomes educated, he develops the power of rational thinking. Due to which he gets the knowledge of good and bad and the ability to take decisions. Only educated people can form an organization by binding in the thread of unity. There is strength in organization as well as the ability to struggle.[4] According to Baba Saheb, education is that which makes a person fearless, teaches the lesson of unity, makes people aware of their rights, teaches them to struggle and teaches them to fight for freedom.

Objective of education

According to Baba Saheb, the objective of education should also be character building. For the development of society, it is necessary for its members to be of good character because only a person with good character will use his knowledge for the welfare of the society. Developing a scientific outlook should also be the objective of education. So that students can solve their problems through research and can analyse facts and ideas by going to the bottom of them and also provide facts. The objective of education is to develop a person mentally and intellectually as well as to destroy social slavery, achieve economic development and political freedom. The real objective of education is to remove the inferiority complex created in the lower class, which stops their progress and makes them slaves.

Education is an effective weapon to fight slavery

He clearly believed that education is the main cause of slavery and education is the most effective weapon to break the shackles of slavery. According to Babasaheb Dr. Ambedkar, mental development of a person is not possible without education. He had said that, "Just as hunger does not provide nutrition to the body and man becomes weak and short-lived, similarly in the absence of education man becomes foolish and becomes a slave of others. Education is the science of developing a person mentally and intellectually, destroying social slavery, achieving economic development and political freedom. Depriving a person or a group of education is denying his existence as a human being and destroying his potential". In his view, higher education is the only cure for all social evils. Babasaheb Dr. Ambedkar believed that to get rights people will have to fight, to fight one will have to study and if one goes to fight without studying, then defeat will be certain.

Education is the milk of a lioness, whoever drinks it will roar

Dr. Ambedkar was a great advocate of education. He had a high degree of attachment with education, because he considered education to be the most important qualification for the development of a person. He believed that, "Education is the milk of a lioness, whoever drinks it will roar" i.e. by drinking the milk of the lioness of education, a person gets the ability to speak, argue and raise questions. This quote of his was equally important for men as well as women, which had a clear message that education creates tremendous self-confidence in a person and an educated person is capable of speaking his mind. He believed that an educated person can fearlessly speak his truth because he has the weapon of education. He had stressed that "Education is the milk of a lioness, whoever drinks it will roar". He used to tell people to educate their women and children. Make them ambitious. Put this thing in their mind that it is their destiny to become great. Greatness can be achieved only through struggle and sacrifice. He clearly believed that women will not benefit from any divine or godly miracle, for their progress women will have to study and struggle in an organized manner. He told women that their salvation lies not in fasting, pilgrimages and pilgrimages but in political power. "Be educated, be organised, struggle" was his main slogan which was enough to make women strong.

Special emphasis on women education

Dr Ambedkar considered illiteracy a curse and considered education to be the most important for the progress of the individual and society. He believed that, "Knowledge and education are not only for men; they are necessary for women also". Therefore, education should be everyone's right and the doors of schools should be open to all without any caste or gender discrimination. He himself had struggled a lot for education and he did not want anyone to be deprived of education. Thus, he laid special emphasis on women's education along with male education. He found education, inter-caste marriage and inter-caste dining as the ways which can end the caste system and patriarchy maintained through endogamy. When he was at Columbia University, he wrote to a friend on the need to educate the depressed classes, especially women. He clearly underlined that, "We will soon see good days and if male education is promoted along with female education, our progress will be greatly accelerated".[5]

Girl education is a father's greatest duty

Dr. Ambedkar stressed that the first duty of a father should be to ensure that the women in his home are not deprived of education. The biggest reason why women feel like slaves after marriage is illiteracy. If women are educated, they will never feel this way.[6] Obviously, Dr. Ambedkar was a strong advocate of women's education and he considered the progress of society impossible without the progress of women. Therefore, he laid special emphasis on the progress of women for which he considered educating women to be extremely important.

'Be educated, be organised, Agitate'

He not only carried forward the ideology of women education of his political guru Mahatma Jyotiba Phule but also strongly supported it and also promoted education considering it important for women empowerment, which is proved by his most famous quote 'Be educated, be organised, struggle'. Dr. Ambedkar himself was a supporter of girl education, and at the same time, he also took important inspiration from Mahatma Jyotiba Phule and Savitribai Phule and laid special emphasis on women education. He taught his life partner Mata Ramabai at home and it is believed that when fundamentalists poured acid on his right hand as part of a conspiracy so that Dr. Ambedkar could not appear for his examination, Mata Ramabai herself wrote the examination of one of his subjects.[7]

Considered women education necessary for the progress of the country

Dr. Ambedkar considered women education necessary for the progress of the country. While young Ambedkar was pursuing his studies in New York, he wrote a letter to his father stressing the need for women's education, saying that "we will soon see good days and if male education is promoted along with female education, our progress will be much faster..." On 18 July 1927, Dr. Ambedkar addressed a meeting of about three thousand women of the Dalit class, where he said, "I measure the progress of the community by the degree of progress achieved by women."

He firmly believed in the fact that if "a woman is educated, a family is educated". He not only encouraged them to educate themselves but also to educate their children and keep them away from all kinds of evils. He strongly opposed the consumption of intoxicants as he realized that most cases of domestic violence occur under their influence. He believed that education is a means of progress as well as self-reliance and women can develop themselves through education. Education as the main objective of his political party 'Independent Labour Party'. Dr. Ambedkar's vision was very clear about women education and he was very confident about the emancipation and progress of women. He believed that *we shall see better days soon and our progress will be greatly accelarated if male education is persuaded side by side with female education.*[8]

Even as a politician, Babasaheb Dr. Ambedkar kept education at the centre of politics. The main objectives that he had adopted for his political party 'Independent Labour Party' were - to implement free and compulsory education, spread and expand adult education, understand the importance of technical education, send people abroad for higher education at government expense for deserving students of backward classes and open new regional universities by reorganizing provincial universities, etc. Dr. Ambedkar opposed the privatization of education due to which education was becoming expensive. He believed that education is not something that can be purchased. It is a process or flow that should be brought within the reach of every person. Therefore, this should be the policy of the departments. His objective was also to keep higher education as cheap and accessible as possible. So that education can be within the reach of every person and no education lover, including women, can be deprived of education due to its being expensive.

Dr. Ambedkar laid special emphasis on the need for education for men and women of all classes so that their social and economic status can increase. All people should get enough education so that they can at least read and write. Therefore, to fulfill this dream of Dr. Ambedkar, it is necessary that education should be free or very cheap. The policy of the government should be such that education is as cheap and accessible as possible for everyone and all women and men can get education of their choice without any hindrance. Caste, sex, religion and poverty should not become a hindrance in the education of any person. But, it is a matter of concern that in today's era education, especially higher education, has become very expensive. Privatization of education is a barrier between poor children and education because it makes education expensive and poor people cannot afford expensive education. As a result, it is becoming difficult for poor people to provide proper education to their children.

Reference

1. https://www.dhammabharat.com/dr-ambedkar-quotes-on-education-in-hindi/

2. Geeta, V. (29 October 2017). "Opening the Library: Babasaheb Ambedkar and his world of books". The Wire.

3. Gaikwad, Dr. Gyanraj Kashinath (2016). Mahamanav Dr. Bhimrao Ramji Ambedkar (in Marathi). Riya Publications. P. 186.

4. S. K. Mahto*, Rani Mahto, in Journal of Advances and Scholarly Researches in Allied Education | Multidisciplinary Academic Research

5. Mathew, Thomas. (1991) Ambedkar: Reform or Revolution, Segment Books, New Delhii.

6.https://www.haribhoomi.com/dr%20ambedkar%20role%20women%20empowerment?infinitescroll=1)

7. Mahanayak Dr. Ambedkar, Serial, &TV

8. Minara Yeasmin (2018) Dr. B.R. Ambedkar's Vision for Women Empowerment, IJCRT, Volume 6, Issue 2 April 2018.

CHAPTER V

Strong Struggle for Women's Liberation and Participation

Babasaheb Dr Bhimrao Ramji Ambedkar was a natural feminist thinker because he had suffered the pain of inequality and discrimination since his childhood. Therefore, he was a strong advocate of gender equality along with caste equality since his student days. Since he was a humanist and sensitive personality, he laid special emphasis on the empowerment of the oppressed, deprived, backward and women. Along with the empowerment of the untouchables, women empowerment was not only the dream of his life but also the main objective. He made significant efforts to take the society on the path of freedom, equality and fraternity. He was a great scholar, institution builder, economic theorist and a great feminist thinker. Dr Ambedkar believed that true democracy will come only when women will get an equal share in ancestral property and they will be given equal rights as men. He firmly believed that the progress of women will be possible only when they will get equal status in the family and society. Education and economic progress will help them achieve social equality.

Dr Ambedkar, since childhood, was deeply concerned about the pitiable and deplorable condition of women in society. He believed deeply in the emancipation and empowerment of women. Since childhood, he was in favour of equal education and opportunity for all, including women. He fought vigorously for the emancipation of women and their social, economic and political participation along with the emancipation of untouchables. Undoubtedly, some Brahmin social reformers played an important role in women's emancipation, mainly Raja Ram Mohan Roy, Ishwar Chandra Vidyasagar etc. However, their main focus was on the social evils related to women and they attacked more on Sati Pratha and the hardships of widowhood. These efforts also freed widows from Sati Pratha to a large extent. But, women could get education, economic independence and participation in political rights only as a result of the struggle of non-Brahmin reformist thinkers and warriors. To understand the principles of the non-brahmanic concept of women's liberation, it is important to understand the thoughts of Dr. Ambedkar. Dr. Ambedkar's thoughts and struggle related to women's liberation are as follows.

Fight for women's liberation and their empowerment

It would not be an exaggeration to say that Dr. Ambedkar was the biggest supporter of women's rights and women's liberation. From childhood, she was very concerned about the pitiable and shameful condition of women in society. He sincerely believed in the liberation and empowerment of women. Dr. Ambedkar believed in the power of women and their role in the process of social reform. He said that every girl who gets married must stand by her husband, claim to be her husband's friend and equal and refuse to be his slave. I am sure that if you follow this advice, you will achieve respect and glory. He strongly advocated family planning measures for women in the Bombay Legislative Assembly. Dr. Ambedkar's work for women was not limited to social reforms but he also used the legal framework to give equal rights to women.[1]

A Strong Voice for Eliminating Anti-Women Practices

Babasaheb raised his voice against degrading practices like child marriage and Devdasi Pratha to inspire helpless women to stand up and fight. In 1928, a women's welfare organization was established in Mumbai, whose president was Babasaheb's wife Ramabai. On 20 January 1942, the All India Dalit Women's Conference was organized under the chairmanship of Dr. Bhim Rao Ambedkar in which about 25 thousand women participated. At that time, the unity of such a large number of women was a big thing. Baba Saheb had praised Dalit women and said, "Women have an unshakable faith in awakening. Women can play a major role in eradicating social evils. I am telling this from my own experience that when I took up the task of Dalit society, I had decided that women should also be taken forward along with men. The amount of progress made by women society, I count it in the progress of Dalit society".[2]

Gender discrimination must be eliminated for social change

Dr. Ambedkar believed that gender discrimination must be eliminated for social change. Dr. Ambedkar adopts an anti-patriarchal stance in the creation of the Hindu Code Bill. He opposes the anti-Shudra and anti-women law of Manusmriti because it makes women subservient and slaves. He likes Buddhist, non-Brahminical tradition because it gives freedom to women and gives them access to knowledge. He believes that any social change is incomplete until gender discrimination is eliminated in that society. Like Mahatma Jyotiba Phule, Dr. Ambedkar considers the caste system to be the main reason for the subordination of women and Dr.

Ambedkar calls upon the people to revolt against this system. Caste System as the Enemy of Equality and Women Empowerment

Dr. Ambedkar saw the caste system as the main enemy of equality and women empowerment. At the same time, he saw exploitative systems as responsible for women's subordination. He emphasised caste-based exploitation and traced the relationship between caste-based exploitation and women's subordination and explained how castes emerged through the regulation of women. In short, he argues that women are the gateway to the caste system.

Attack on the Caste System and Patriarchy

Dr. Ambedkar believed in the end of capitalism because capitalism also exploits and reinforces patriarchy. But he believed that women's subordination would not automatically end with the end of capitalism. Dr. Ambedkar argues that for this purpose the caste system and patriarchy must be attacked. Women's subordination cannot end in a caste-based society and therefore women must lead the struggle for the abolition of castes. He sees an organic connection between the struggle against the caste system and the struggle for women's liberation. Thus the idea of women's liberation is an inherent part of his ideology and is not a symbolic addition.

Transforming private matters of women into political issues

He tried to bring into the public sphere under the aegis of the legal system the atrocities which women had to face privately within the confines of the home. Issues like bigamy, maintenance etc. are all brought into public debate. He wants to transform private matters into political issues and for this he has drafted the Hindu Code Bill. His journey of codifying the law is to limit the private sphere and make the public sphere more comprehensive. Women's right to share in property, right to seek divorce and marry as per their wish, all these issues have come up in the Bill and stand in opposition to the prevalent familial abuse of women. In the political sphere too, he was opposed to private ownership of land and was in favour of its socialisation. Thus, his views on political issues are in line with the question of women.[3]

Special emphasis on women's organization

Dr. Ambedkar laid special emphasis on women's organization, he believed that if women get organized, they can make an important contribution in giving the right direction to the society. He used to emphasize on educating women to improve the education system of India. He was well aware of women power, struggle, courage, sacrifice and self-denial.[4]

Open support for women's franchise

Dr. Ambedkar was a great advocate of the democratic system and adult franchise. He openly supported adult franchise which meant to provide voting rights to women along with men. In other words, Dr. Ambedkar not only advocated strongly for the right to vote for women but also ensured it through the Constitution of India. Adult franchise was Dr. Ambedkar's idea for which he fought from the Simon Commission in 1928 till later. It was opposed at that time. At that time, there was a debate on giving voting rights to women in Europe and blacks in America. Ambedkar took forward the issue of the right to vote. He warned the members of the electoral assembly not to compromise on the basic principles of democracy in their eagerness to bring the Indian states together. Dr. Ambedkar chose a democracy of rights for the new India instead of a democracy based on protection.[5]

Dr. Ambedkar was not satisfied with a little change in the status of women, but he was an advocate of radical change in the lives of women. Therefore, he laid special emphasis on women's education, economic independence and participation in political rights. He kept women empowerment along with the exploited and deprived at the center of his pen and speech and always raised his voice for women's rights. It would not be an exaggeration to say that the life and philosophy of Dr. Ambedkar proved to be a boon for human rights and for the liberation of the exploited, deprived and women of India. He struggled for the welfare of humanity from the beginning of his life to the end of his life. They wanted to ensure not only social equality between man and man but also equal status and dignity between men and women.

Reference

1. Shambunath (2018): Dr. BR Ambedkar and women empowerment in India, International Journal of Academic Development, ISSN: 2455-4197, Volume 3; Issue 1; Page No. 1392-1394 1. also see www.academicsjournal.com

2.https://theshudra.com/dr-ambedkar/know-about-the-champion-of-women-rights-in-india-dr- ambedkar-on- international-womens-day/

3. https://theleaflet.in/dr-babasaheb-ambedkar-and-the-question-of-womens-liberation-in-india-iii/

4. Dr. Naaj Paraveen, baaba saaheb aur hindoo kod bil: mahilaon kee dasha sudhaarane mein meel ka patthar bana ek kadam (https://www.amarujala.com/columns/blog/hindu-code-bill-dr-babasaheb-ambedkar-significance-importance-nehru-and- the-hindu-code-

bill)

5.https://navbharattimes.indiatimes.com/nazaria-dr-ambedkar-wanted-to-give-women-right- to/articleshow/17493392.cms

CHAPTER VI

Progress of women: The Main Parameter for the Development of the Community

Babasaheb Dr. Ambedkar laid great emphasis on the development of women. He believed that no community or society can develop without the development of women, because the population of women is half of the total population of the country. The development of women is also very important to make the society strong and developed. In other words, it can be understood that Dr. Ambedkar believed in the power of women and their role in the process of social reform. According to Dr. Ambedkar, the progress of women is the main parameter for the development of the community. He linked the progress of the society and the country with the progress of women and considered the progress of the country incomplete without the progress of women.

A great supporter of gender equality

Dr. Ambedkar wanted equality and social justice not only for men but also for women. Therefore, he was a great supporter of gender equality. His concept of equality was not limited to men only but he was also a strong supporter of equality of women. He believed that no society can develop as long as the women of that society are backward. He was a strong supporter of women empowerment in all spheres of life and openly revolted against all the oppressive customs of Hindu society for the betterment of women. Although his protest was peaceful and non-violent, he achieved amazing successes. His dream was to bring gender equality in all areas of society which has not yet been fully realized. Therefore, until complete gender equality is established, the relevance of his ideas will remain. His ideas support women empowerment along with social reconstruction. Dr. Ambedkar expressed concern over the pitiable condition of women. He emphasized that women should be treated equally and given equal respect.

Advocate of all-round development of women

Dr. Ambedkar was in favor of making women self-reliant and empowered in every way. Therefore, he wanted to see women in a leading role in every field which was possible only with their all-round development. His deep concern and feelings for the all-round development of women are reflected in his thoughts. As a true feminist, Dr. Ambedkar's views on the question of women emphasized their right to education, equal treatment with men, right to property and participation in the political process. We can know his feelings and respect for women in his last speech in the Indian Parliament. He quoted the famous thoughts of Daniel O'Connell, an Irish patriot, "No man can be grateful at the cost of his honor, no woman can be grateful at the cost of her chastity. And no nation can be grateful at the cost of its purity."[1]

Progress of women is the main measure of the progress of the community

Babasaheb Dr. Ambedkar was a great supporter of the progress of society, so he believed that the progress of the community or society lies in the progress of women. According to Dr. Ambedkar, the progress of a society depends on the progress of women. Dr. Ambedkar was a great advocate of women's rights as well as women's progress, therefore he had stressed that, "I measure the progress of a community by the degree of progress which women have achieved". This statement of Dr. Ambedkar on the issue of women's development is very important which highlights Babasaheb's thinking and ideology towards women empowerment and their progress. It means that Dr. Ambedkar was a strong supporter of women's participation along with men in the progress of society and was a great supporter of women's participation in the stream of development.

He believed that no society can become developed without the development of women. Women constitute half the population of the society, without their development how can we think about the development of the community i.e. the country. In other words, it can be said that Dr. Ambedkar clearly believed that without the progress of women, the progress of society cannot be complete. If women are backward, then the society will also be backward. Dr. Ambedkar considered education important for the development of women. He thought that only through women's education the society will become educated because an educated woman will definitely educate her children too. Undoubtedly, women are progressing in various fields today and are making unprecedented contribution in the progress of society and the country. All this is the result of the thinking of Babasaheb Dr. Ambedkar who not only advocated for women's progress but also being the chief architect of the Constitution of India, opened the doors of their progress by providing all social, economic, political and fundamental rights to women. Husband and wife are each other's friends

Dr Ambedkar considered husband and wife to be each other's friends. He completely rejected the relationship of master and slave. But women are men's allies and not slaves. He insisted that every girl who marries her husband should claim to be her husband's friend and equal, and refuse to be his slave, I am sure that if you follow this advice, you will bring respect and dignity to yourself. He considered men and women to be complementary to each other, which means one without the other is incomplete. That is, to live a social life, a woman without a man is incomplete and a man without a woman is also incomplete.

Strong advocacy of family planning

Dr Ambedkar was also a strong supporter of women's complete social participation and he wanted women to play a decisive role in social and family matters as well. That is, it was Dr Ambedkar's wish to take women out of the complete domination of men. His belief was that women should not surrender completely even in the matter of procreation and they should be given the freedom to take a decision in this regard after thinking carefully. Being a strong feminist thinker, she strongly advocated family planning measures for women in the Bombay Legislative Assembly. She considered the woman's wish to have children as important.[2] Dr. Ambedkar's work for women was not limited to social reforms only, but he also used the legal framework to give equal rights to women.

Concern for the empowerment of Muslim and other women

Dr. Ambedkar was a very egalitarian as well as a highly sensitive thinker and he believed in the liberation of all women and wanted to see every woman empowered. His concept of women empowerment included not only Dalit women but also all women of religions other than Hinduism. That is, he was concerned about the empowerment of not only Hindu women but also all women of Muslim and other religions. In his famous book, "Pakistan-Partition of India", he expressed his views about Muslim women and their religious traditions, wearing of burqa (veil), their marriage, etc. Muslim women were oppressed under various religious traditions. Her views towards all women, irrespective of their religion, caste and class, were humanitarian. She often raised her voice against all kinds of oppression and injustice towards women.[3]

In short, it can be said that Babasaheb Dr. Ambedkar believed that the progress of a community or society lies in the progress of women. He clearly believed that the society in which women develop, that society will also definitely develop. According to Dr. Ambedkar, the progress of a society depends on the progress of women. Dr Ambedkar was also a unique advocate of women's progress who stressed that, "I measure the progress of a community by the degree of progress that women have achieved. As far as women's rights are concerned, Dr Ambedkar's work was not limited to social reforms only, but he also contributed significantly in creating a strong legal framework and ensured women's empowerment through a constitutional provision of equal rights for women. Undoubtedly, his thinking and ideology was very positive and progressive towards women empowerment, as a result of which, being the chief architect of the Constitution of India, he played a wonderful role in ensuring women's rights. However, his wonderful contribution to women is rarely discussed, which is a matter of sadness. And even women themselves are not aware of the contribution made by Babasaheb for them.

References

1. https://www.dailyexcelsior.com/ambedkar-on-women/

2. Shambunath (2018): Dr. BR Ambedkar and women empowerment in India, International Journal of Academic Development, ISSN: 2455-4197, Volume 3; Issue 1; Page No. 1392-1394 1. also see www.academicsjournal.com

3. https://www.dailyexcelsior.com/ambedkar-on-women/

CHAPTER VII

Dr. Ambedkar as Labour Minister: Important Legislative Measures for Women Empowerment

How much Babasaheb Dr Ambedkar was conscious about women rights is evident from his efforts as Labour Minister. As a Labour Minister during the British rule, Dr Ambedkar took important legislative measures for women empowerment which not only simplified the working life of women workers and employees but also ensured their job security. In 1942, being the Labour Minister of the Executive Council of the Governor General, he introduced a Maternity Benefit Bill. He made several provisions in the Constitution for the welfare of women and protection of civil rights. Apart from this, he also highlighted the issues of Muslim women. All workers, especially women workers, should be grateful to Dr. Ambedkar as he introduced many legal measures for women workers in India i.e. enacted several laws like 'Mines Maternity Benefit Act', 'Women Workers Welfare Fund', 'Women and Child Labour Protection Act', 'Maternity Benefit for Women Workers', and 'Restoration of the ban on employment of women on underground work in coal mines'.[1]

Strong advocate of labour interests

Dr. Ambedkar was a strong advocate of labour interests. He was not only the most important Dalit icon and hero for the marginalised and deprived classes in post-independence India, but he also contributed immensely to the labour movement in the country during the British rule. Women were also included in his labour movement. In his 1936 book Annihilation of Caste, Ambedkar writes that "what was inherent in the caste system was not only division of labour, but division of labourers as well". "Now the caste system will not allow Hindus to take up occupations where they wish if they are not genetically theirs." He writes, If a Hindu is seen starving rather than taking up new occupations not allotted to his caste, the reason for this is found in the caste system.

Strong support for the right to strike

The right to strike is a very important right of employees and workers in democratic countries, by using which the employees work to stop their exploitation. Without the right to strike and protest, the employees actually remain only slaves. Dr. Ambedkar understood the importance of strike very well, so he strongly supported the right of employees and workers to strike. Not only this, when he was made the Labor Minister, he openly promoted the interests of employees and workers and as Labor Minister, he also gave legal support to the right to strike.

Dr. Ambedkar opposed the Industry Disputes Bill introduced by the Congress Government of Bombay in 1937, calling it the "Workers‘ Civil Liberties Suspension Act" because it provided for six months' imprisonment for participating in an illegal strike. While opposing the bill in the Assembly in 1938, he argued that punishing workers for participating in a strike was "nothing less than making the employee a slave". He said that slavery is nothing but involuntary servitude.[2]

Desire for women empowerment through reconstruction of Hindu society

Dr. Ambedkar's emphasis was on reconstruction of Hindu society on the basis of equality rather than the social reforms initiated by Brahmo Samaj or Arya Samaj, because their (Brahmo Samaj or Arya Samaj's) efforts were limited only to the upper strata of society. His deep study of Smritis and scriptures and his experience of the reaction of the upper castes during the temple entry movement strengthened his conclusions on Hindu philosophy and society.[3]

On the other hand, Babasaheb Dr. Ambedkar knew Indian society very deeply, especially Hindu society, and was well aware of its inequitable nature. Therefore, he wanted to transform it completely so that the social, economic and political position of women could be strengthened. It is worth noting that the condition of women in Indian society was very pathetic and their empowerment was very important for which it was necessary to completely change the Indian society.

Opposition to the Purdah (veil) system

Dr. Ambedkar was strongly opposed to the Purdah system prevalent in India because Purdah is the first enemy of women's freedom which hides the identity of the woman itself. His secular perspective is known through his views on the "Purdah" (veil) system, religious conversion and legal rights for Muslim women. It means that Babasaheb Dr. Ambedkar was a great advocate of the liberation or freedom of all women, so he wanted that Muslim women should also get freedom and they should also get all the rights that men get.

Right to Maternity Leave (Maternity Leave for Pregnant Working Women)

Today working women can take 26 weeks of maternity leave, which was started by Babasaheb Dr. Ambedkar. On 10 November 1938, Baba Saheb Ambedkar raised the issues related to women's problems in a strong way in the Bombay Legislative Assembly. During this, he expressed his views on the concerns related to women's health during childbirth. Do you know that the first Maternity Benefit Bill was introduced by Dr. Ambedkar in 1942? After this, maternity leave was also provided to women through the Employees' State Insurance Act of 1948. Maternity leave is an important right of every female employee today, which is actually such an important right in the field of women's rights that it has made the working life of women very easy. During maternity leave, women get full salary, which is a very important arrangement from the point of view of women. This right also provides a lot of relief to the male colleagues of women and their families.

Baba Saheb had done this work at a time when even the most powerful countries of that era were far behind in this matter. In a country like America, the way for maternity leave for women was cleared after the intervention of the court in the year 1987. America had officially arranged for paid maternity leave for working women by making Family and Medical Leave Act in the year 1993. But Babasaheb thought ahead and made it a reality.[4]

Provision of 8-hour working day for employees

We should be deeply grateful to Babasaheb Dr. Ambedkar because it was Dr. Ambedkar who, as the Labour Minister, implemented the 8-hour working day in India and reduced it from 14 hours to 8 hours. He brought it in the 7th session of the Indian Labour Conference in New Delhi on 27 November, 1942. This benefit was not only for male employees and workers but also for female employees and workers. Through this law, Dr. Ambedkar definitely freed women from exploitation along with men. In fact, it was Babasaheb's outstanding contribution that brought the employees and workers out of slave-like conditions.

Thus, Dr. Ambedkar, as the Labour Minister, played an important role in the empowerment of the workers and employees of India, which also included women. Undoubtedly, most of the facilities that men and women are getting today as employees are the gift of Babasaheb Dr. Ambedkar, for which all of us employees should be grateful to him and always remember him for his great contribution.

References

1. https://www.ambedkaritetoday.com/2019/11/dr-ambedkar-and-the-rights-of-labourers-in-india.html

2. https://theleaflet.in/the-unknown-ambedkar-indias-first-labour-minister/

3. www.questjournal.org

4.https://theshudra.com/dr-ambedkar/know-about-the-champion-of-women-rights-in-india-dr-ambedkar-on-internation-womens-day/

CHAPTER VIII

A Strong Supporter of Hindu Code Bill and Women' Rights: Resignation from the post of Law Minister

Babasaheb Dr. Ambedkar, a pioneer of social justice, a strong advocate of women's liberation, a determined fighter and a strong feminist scholar, was the first Indian to break the shackles that had held back the process of women's advancement in India for centuries. He made significant efforts to take the society on the path of freedom, equality and fraternity and was fully committed to providing justice to all in all spheres of life without discrimination of caste, colour, religion and sex. With his sincere efforts, he laid the foundation of gender equality, women's liberation and empowerment by codifying the Common Civil Code for Hindus and other sections of Indian society. His sincere efforts for the welfare of women are enough to prove him a great feminist.

Objective of Hindu Code Bill

The objective of the Hindu Code Bill was to break the shackles of slavery of women for centuries in the name of rotten traditions and make them independent and self-reliant like men. Along with caste eradication, women empowerment was also a big dream of Babasaheb Dr. Ambedkar, which he started seeing from his student days itself. Dr. Ambedkar wanted revolutionary changes in the social, economic and political status of Indian women, especially Hindu women, which included both upper caste and Dalit women. To improve their condition, he wanted to make such a law which would work as an effective weapon in improving their social and legal status. Therefore, to fulfill this objective, he made the 'Hindu Code' bill in favor of all women. Both this Hindu Code Bill and Dr. Ambedkar had to face fierce opposition from the fundamentalists. On the "Hindu Code Bill", Durgabai Deshmukh, Member of Lok Sabha, Mrs. Padamji Naidu, Rajshree, Mrs. Chandrakala, Urmila Mehta, Mrs. Mithan, Minister of Mahila Congress, Kumari Mukul and their women's group went from village to village and city to city with Dr. Ambedkar and painted the picture of the social and economic plight of Indian women in meetings and public gatherings. Attacking the male-dominated culture, this bill gave Indian women the same legal rights as men and made them proud. Due to this bill, Hindu women were given the same rights as men in marriage, divorce, etc. Eight acts were made in this bill.

1. Hindu Marriage Act.
2. Special Marriage Act.
3. Adoption, Minority Protection Act.
4. Hindu Succession Act.
5. Maintenance of Weak and Resourceless Family Members Act.
6. Minor Protection Act.
7. Succession Act.
8. Hindu Widow Remarriage Rights Act.
9. Rights in Father's Property etc. in Hindu Code Bill.

The Hindu Code Bill was not only an important document but also a decisive weapon to empower women by making laws on various aspects related to women especially like marriage, widow's right to remarriage, divorce, succession, adoption, rights in father's property. According to the Hindu Code Bill, marriage of a girl or boy of any caste i.e. inter-caste marriage was not illegal. According to the Hindu Code, a wife and husband could marry only once at a time. If a husband marries while his first wife is alive and a wife marries while her first husband is alive, then he will be punished by law. The Hindu Code made a rule to give a Hindu woman a share or portion in the husband's property equal to that of her children after the death of the husband. There was no provision for a widow to remarry in Hindu religious scriptures, nor did she get any share or portion in the property. By the grace of the Hindu Code, after the death of the father, the daughter was also made the heir of the property equal to the brothers. Similarly, the right to adopt was available only to a child born from one's own clan, but according to the Code, a girl or boy born in any Hindu family could be adopted and that boy or girl, irrespective of the Hindu caste they belong to, become the heir of the property of the person being adopted. The interesting thing was that now not only a boy could be adopted, but a girl could also be adopted. Therefore, in short, it can be said that the Hindu Code had destroyed the old religious bastion of the Hindus.[1]

Strong supporter of radical legal changes in the status of women

By passing the Hindu Code Bill, Dr. Ambedkar wanted to bring radical legal changes in the status of women. Through the Hindu Code Bill, the social and economic status of women in the family and society should be strengthened, so he kept the status of a daughter equal to that of a son and the status of a wife equal to that of a husband. The Hindu Code Bill was definitely an important measure to empower women, the aim of which was to make women self-reliant and capable of living a dignified life. Although the Hindu Code Bill could not be passed in its original form, but in the later years almost all its provisions had to be implemented by the governments one after the other, which brought revolutionary changes in the lives of women. Today women have got most of the rights and powers that Babasaheb Dr. Ambedkar wanted to give them. In true sense, this is the victory of Babasaheb's ideas and his feminism thinking which was imbued with the ideology of women empowerment.

Now, in case of divorce, the husband will have to pay alimony to his wife and in property division, the daughter will get equal share as the son. Women can also adopt a child of their own choice. On getting the right to adopt a child, women who did not have children will get relief from the mental and physical harassment given by the family and society. Dr. Ambedkar believed that he wanted to do welfare of the entire women of India by getting the Hindu Code Bill passed. During the days when the Hindu Code Bill was being considered, he had seen many young women and adult women belonging to the upper castes who were abandoned by their cruel, tyrannical, alcoholic, butcher and immoral husbands, who had been abandoned by their husbands and were given a nominal monthly alimony of four to five rupees for their living. Often the husbands did not even give this much allowance. These abandoned women were forced to live a life of slavery and poverty. Seeing the pitiable condition of these women, their parents and brothers were also sad. Because there was no law to end the suffering of these abandoned women.

The Hindu Code Bill was the only law that could stand in favor of such helpless, sad and oppressed women. What I mean to say is that the Hindu Code Bill was a law that brought about a radical change in the worrisome condition of Indian women. In which there was a provision of punishment for the culprits in favor of women who were oppressed in any form and situation in the society. Through this bill, Dr. Ambedkar and his women companions were trying for legal reforms and rights in the condition of women. In support of the Hindu Code Bill, a council was organized in Bhandari Hall of Dadar on 21 August 1949, in which 25 women organizations and 10 social organizations submitted a memorandum to the government in support of the Hindu Code Bill. On 19 January 1950 at 05:30 in Wilson College, Urmila Mehta and Mrs. Mithan strongly supported the

Hindu Code Bill through their fiery speeches. This movement continued for about 5 years in which many Dalit and non-Dalit women joined. The purpose of this movement was to get social justice which had been violated for years.[2]

Some excerpts from the debate in the Constituent Assembly on the Hindu Code Bill

Various members of the Constituent Assembly expressed their views on the Hindu Code Bill, to which Law Minister Dr. Ambedkar gave clear answers. Some excerpts from the debate are quoted below which highlight the social and political views regarding the opposition and support of the bill.

Smt. Hansa Mehta (Bombay General) speaking on the bill argued: Mr. Chairman, I congratulate the Honorable Minister for bringing this bill even at such a late date in the session. I also congratulate or express gratitude to Sir B.N. Rau and his colleagues for the great hard work done for the report on which these recommendations are based. This Bill codifying Hindu law is a revolutionary Bill and though we are not entirely satisfied with it, it will prove to be a great milestone in the social history of the Hindus. But since the drafting of this Bill many things have happened and one of the greatest things is the achievement of our political independence. Our new Constitution is being framed; we have already agreed on the fundamental principles on which this new Constitution is to be drafted. The new State will be a democratic State and democracy is based on the equality of individuals. From this point of view we will now have to consider the problems of succession and marriage etc. which are before us. Therefore, the Select Committee will have to see that the new Bill is by 6 p.m. framed on these principles.

It is true that the Code has abolished six discriminations in respect of inheritance. A woman is recognised as an heir and is also entitled to enjoy her property with full rights; that is, the Code has abolished the limited property rights of woman. Still we feel that the matter does not go far enough. A daughter who is considered an heir inherits the property, but she inherits only half of the son's share. This is a violation of the principle of equality on which we have repeatedly stated that our new Constitution is going to be based, a Constitution that aims to ensure social, political and economic justice for the people of this country. So we believe that a daughter should get an equal share as a son in her father's property and a son should also get an equal share as a daughter in his mother's property.

It is also argued that a daughter gets a share from her father as well as from her husband, while a man gets nothing from his wife. We have already proposed, that is the women's organisations have said, that a husband can also inherit his wife's property in the same way as a wife inherits her husband's property. There is already a provision for husband's inheritance in the Indian Succession Act and I think we would do well to copy that provision.

People have argued, and the honourable friend who spoke before me has said, that if a daughter is given her share, particularly in landed property, there will be fragmentation of land. But why is this argument put forward in the case of a daughter's inheritance? The same thing applies when a man has more than one son; if he has, say, four or five sons, the land will have to be fragmented; Why was this argument not raised then, and why is it raised only when the question of daughters inheriting property arises? The better thing would be to have a law against fragmentation and sell off the property if it falls below a certain limit. Or there is another option and that is collectivisation of land. Then on the question of marriage I am satisfied, and the women of India will be very happy to know that the principle of monogamy has been recognised, and if the Code comes into being the principle of monogamy will be established.

Sir, we have realised that all civilised nations, all civilised communities have adopted the principle of monogamy. I think all the disrespect towards women and all the atrocities on women are due to the fact that the principle of polygamy exists. If we had monogamy, I do not think women would be kidnapped, married off or other things would be done to them. It is a very good principle and I hope the House will accept it. But there are one or two points which I would like to suggest regarding some of the conditions of marriage. As regards the marriage of sapindas and the definition of sapinda, it needs a little modification; we are not at all satisfied with the definition given in the Code. Again, we would like that the age of marriage should also be a condition for a valid marriage. We have got the Sarda Act but that is not satisfactory, people are not satisfied with it because it is not able to prevent child marriage; it is not effective. For this reason we would like the law to be more stringent. If we want the age of marriage to be sixteen years, it is very necessary that it should be included as one of the conditions for a valid marriage and I would like the Select Committee to make this change. Then as regards divorce, from the point of view of some people that also does not go far enough. However, there is one thing which I would like to bring to the notice of the Members of the Select Committee and that is the time given for divorce.

The Honourable Dr. B. R. Ambedkar: (Responding to the arguments and questions of Shrimati Hansa Mehta and other fellow members)

Mr. President, my task has been made much lighter by the fact that the Bill has received such substantial support from this House. I shall, therefore, confine myself to answering some of the points raised by the speakers who took part in this debate.

I shall begin with the remarks made by my honourable friend, Mr. Naziruddin Ahmad. Sir, I thought that the Legislature is not an institution and a Member of this House, who is a lawyer, certainly does not come here to practise or to plead. But somehow my friend, either for a fee or out of pure generosity, undertook the task of representing the views of some of his clients who perhaps did not have the courage to speak their minds. I shall, however, not raise any technical objection but consider the points he has raised.

Sir, his complaint was that the Bill was not given adequate publicity and that the public was not given adequate opportunity to weigh the importance of the measure. I should have thought that the clients of my honourable friend had misinformed him on this point. This Bill had its origin in a law which came into effect in the year 1937. Since that year the provisions of this Bill have been passed around from one side to the other, from one Committee to another. For example, in the year 1941, the Home Department appointed a Committee to consider certain difficulties arising out of the Women's Property Rights Act, 1937, to report on the difficulties and to suggest remedies. This Committee, known as the Rau Committee, submitted its report on June 19, 1941. My honourable friend, had he referred to this report, would have seen the publicity the Committee gave to its proposals, the questionnaires it issued, the statements it received, the witnesses it examined and the travels it made from one Province to another to ascertain the opinion of the local public.

Again in 1942 the same Committee presented two draft Bills, one on succession and the other on marriage. The Hindu Succession Bill was introduced in the Assembly in 1943. It was referred to a Joint Committee of both Houses. That Joint Committee again invited public opinion and a volume of them was collected and circulated in the then Legislature. Keeping all this in mind, I am sure that the statement of my honourable friend that the Government has not given sufficient publicity cannot be accepted as true. He also referred to a report called the Minority Report of Justice Mitter in which he has analysed the pros and cons of the various points included in this Bill. Sir, I do not like to say anything derogatory about a member of a Committee who has done so much useful work, but I cannot help saying that this member literally ran away from his own opinion. If my honourable friend Mr. Naziruddin Ahmad reads the majority report, he will find that all the proposals in that Bill giving rights to women were actually based on a publication published in the year 1930 by this member of the Committee. In that book he had propounded the view that the case law restricting the rights of women had no basis. After all, for the very reasons best known to him, he did not say that this argument has no merit.

My honourable friend also referred to the fact that this Bill is after all confined to property other than agricultural land. The conclusion which he drew from that fact was that this codification was only a partial codification, because a large part of the property which is the subject of inheritance is felt to be untouched by the provisions of this Bill. Sir, there are two explanations for the non-inclusion of agricultural property*. My honourable friend, if he refers to the Schedules of the Government of India Act, where the subject-matter of legislation for the Union and the Provinces is prescribed, will find that land is placed in the "Provincial List". As a result of the judicial interpretation given by the Federal Court it was held that the word "land" or the item "land", which is included in the "Provincial List", covers not only tenancy land but also succession to land and consequently any provision made by the Central Legislature in respect of succession to land would be extra-territorial. In order that this may not happen, the Committee very deliberately kept agricultural land free from the provisions of this Bill. But what I would like to say is something different. I should have thought that rather than being a defect or fault in the Bill, the exclusion of land from this Bill was perhaps an advantage because I believe there is no necessity that a uniform law of inheritance should apply to all kinds of property.

Property varies in its nature, varies in its importance in the social life of the community and consequently it may not be of any small advantage to society to have one set of laws of inheritance for agricultural property and another set of laws for non-agricultural property.

Property, it may be that on a better consideration of the situation, Indian or Hindu society may come to the conclusion that land which is the basis of its economic life would be better governed by the law of primogeniture so that neither the youngest sons nor females can inherit it. As to the share in inheritance, as I said, the question being left open would be of advantage to society in that it would be able to consider the matter afresh. I do not, therefore, consider that the remarks made by my honourable friend in regard to this Bill are really an apology.

As for my friend Mr. Chaudhuri, he regards this legislation as a communal legislation. I agree that in so far as it refers to Hindu society, which is one of the many communities living in this country, in a logical sense it may be called a piece of communal legislation. But what is the alternative? If the alternative of my honourable friend was that there should not be communal laws of inheritance and communal laws of marriage, but a uniform civil code, applicable to all classes, all communities, all individuals: indeed to citizens without any distinction on the basis of religion, creed or caste, I am certainly at one with him. That is not, of course, his conclusion. His conclusion is, if I understand him, that this law, owing to the fact that in the past the view was expressed that the future society here described would be secular, has no right to legislate for the secular community: that would be a most disastrous conclusion. There are so many communities inhabiting this country. Each has its own special laws and merely because the State wishes to assume a secular character it should withdraw itself from regulating the lives of the various communities, that would undoubtedly lead to nothing but anarchy and chaos. I am certainly not prepared to sign such a resolution myself.

His second remark was that the Bill does not take into account customary law. He referred to certain decisions of the Privy Council. I should have thought that it was unnecessary to refer to the authority of the Privy Council at this time of the day because it is well established by a long series of decisions that custom will override the text so far as Hindus are concerned. "Mrs. We all know that. But what are we doing? What we are doing is this. We are preventing the growth of new customs. We are not destroying existing customs. We are recognising existing customs because these rules of law are the result of customs prevailing in Hindu society. They have been born of customs and we think they have now become so strong that we can actually give them flesh and life in the body politic by our legislation. Then my friend Dr. Sitaramayya asked me whether the rule of law contained in this Bill, under which women will acquire an absolute state in their inherited property, will apply to widows who have already taken up the property before the passing of the Act. I am afraid I must do so. He says that this Bill has no retrospective effect.

Nor will it be possible to give retrospective effect to the principles of the absolute property of women for the simple reason that long before this Bill comes into existence, vested rights in that property would have been created and it would not be right and proper to divest them of their property, no matter how much sympathy we may have for the widow.

Shrimati Hansa Mehta raised a number of questions which indicated that women and particularly herself are not satisfied with some of the provisions relating to women's rights in this Bill. It may be that in the ideal sense this Bill may not live up to expectations. But I would like to tell them that they must remember that this society is a passive society. Hindu society has always believed that law-making is the work of God or memory and that Hindu society has no right to change the law. That being so, the law in Hindu society will remain the same for generations to come. Society has never acknowledged its power and its responsibility in moulding its social, economic and legal life. This is the first time that we are exhorting Hindu society to take such a big step and I have not the slightest doubt in my mind that a society which has courage enough to endure the big step which we are asking it to take on the basis of reason in this Bill, will not hesitate to proceed on the path which it has yet to tread and to reach the goal which it has in mind.

Sir, much has been said about the fact that the overwhelming majority of public opinion is against this Bill. Of course I have not gone into the opinions which we have received, but I wish to say that this is hardly a question which we can decide by counting heads. This is not a question which we can decide according to the opinion of the majority. When society is in a transitory state of change, leaving the past and moving towards the future, there are of course conflicting considerations: one pulls towards the past and one pulls towards the future and the test which we apply is no more than a test of one's conscience. I have not the slightest doubt in my mind that the provisions of this will are in accord with the conscience of the community, and therefore, even as a matter of fact, I have no hesitation in putting forward this measure. The majority of the people of our country do not approve of it. Mr. President, the question is:

"That the Bill to amend and codify certain branches of Hindu Law be referred to a Select Committee consisting of Mr. Alladi Krishnaswami Aiyar, Dr. Bakshi Tek Chand, Mr. M.A. Aiyangar, Mrs. G. Durgabai, Mr. L. Krishnaswami Bharati, Mr. U. Srinivasa Mallya, Mr. Mihir Lal

Chattopadhyay, Dr. P.S. Deshmukh, Mrs. Renuka Ray, Dr. P.K. Sen, Babu Ram Narayan Singh, Mr. Kishori Mohan Tripathi, Mrs. Ammu Swaminathan, Pandit Balakrishna Sharma, Mr. Khurshid Lal, Siri Brajeshwar Prasad, Mr. B. Siva Rao, Mr. Baldev Sharoop, Mr. V.C. Keshava Rao and the mover with directions to report not later than the last day of the first week of the next session of the Assembly and the number of members required to constitute one meeting of the Committee shall be five." The motion was adopted.[3]

Strong opposition to the Bill by Hindu orthodoxies

Strong opposition to the Hindu Code Bill by Hindu orthodoxies He made every possible effort to stop this bill from becoming a reality. The more progressive steps Babasaheb took for the progress of Indian women, the more the fundamentalists tried to pull him back. Dr. Ambedkar had to face personal insults many times in protest against the Hindu Code Bill. Stones were even pelted at his house and he was boycotted in the Parliament. Along with Dr. Ambedkar, many Dalit and non-Dalit women fought the social and economic battle of Indian women to get the "Hindu Code Bill" passed. Irritated by a progressive step like the Code Bill, the fundamentalists spread a web of animosity, hatred and tension against Dr. Ambedkar all around. Often, the Hindu Code Bill discussion meetings organized by Dr. Ambedkar and his women colleagues were directly attacked by the fundamentalists, and the discussion meetings were forcibly closed.

Finally, when the 'Hindu Code Bill' could not be passed in the Parliament, Dr. Ambedkar resigned from the Parliament in protest. The opposition to the bill by Hindu orthodox and the dramatic step taken by Prime Minister Jawaharlal Nehru greatly disappointed Dr. Ambedkar, who was the then Law Minister. However, he resisted the opposition democratically and decided to resign. Saddened and angered by the attack of orthodox Hindus on women's interests and social justice, Dr. Ambedkar resigned from his post of Law Minister. This was a huge and historic step taken by Dr. Ambedkar in support of women's interest and empowerment.
Opposition to Hindu Code Bill by Media

Dr Ambedkar did not get any support from the media of that time. Instead of support, newspapers were also publishing many provocative articles against the Hindu Code Bill. At that time, the atmosphere of the country had become toxic against Dr Ambedkar and his women colleagues, which the media further increased. But, Dr Ambedkar and his colleagues stood firm and continued the fight till the end. Ultimately, orthodox religious leaders, traditional Hindus, irresponsible media and the indifferent attitude of Prime Minister Nehru proved to be obstacles in the path of the Hindu Code Bill, due to which Dr Ambedkar had to face great disappointment.

Dr Ambedkar's resignation from the post of Law Minister for women's rights

When the Hindu Code Bill was introduced in Parliament in 1948 and debated on the floor of the House, the opposition strongly opposed the bill. As Law Minister, Dr. Ambedkar tried his level best to defend the Bill by pointing out the shortcomings of Indian society and argued that the ideals in the Bill were based on the constitutional principles of equality, liberty and fraternity and that the Indian society, which is characterised by the caste system, oppression of women and denial of equality to them, required a legal framework for a social transformation in which women have equal rights as men. He also stated that the Bill was intended to codify the rules of Hindu Law which are scattered in innumerable decisions of the High Courts and the General Council and which are a matter of terror to the common man.[4]

Babasaheb Dr. Ambedkar fought hard on many fronts for the Hindu Code Bill. On the one hand he was fighting against the conservatives and orthodox forces and on the other hand, as the Law Minister, he was taking on the government and the opposition. He was facing criticism from all sides and in this task the media was also raising the flag of opposition to the Hindu Code Bill. The inequality-ridden society and powers did not want to see the doors of women's liberation open in any way. Ultimately, when the 'Hindu Code Bill' could not be passed in the Parliament, Dr. Ambedkar resigned from the Parliament in protest. Dr. Ambedkar was deeply disappointed by the dramatic step taken by Prime Minister Jawaharlal Nehru instead of the opposition of Hindu conservatives. Despite this, Dr. Ambedkar democratically opposed those opposing the Hindu Code Bill and resigned from his post of Union Law Minister. Undoubtedly, this was an unprecedented and historic step taken by Dr. Ambedkar in support of women's interest and empowerment. Dr. Ambedkar's resignation reflects his solid fight against depriving women of rights and ignoring their interests. In fact, no one has taken such a big step for women's interests before and after Babasaheb. That is, no one has given up a big post like the Union Law Minister for women's rights. The women of India should always remember this sacrifice and contribution of Babasaheb and remain grateful to him.

References

1. Hindu Code Bill and Ambedkar-Sohanlal Shastri Vidya Vachaspati

2. Anita Bharati (Anita Bharati is a well-known Dalit writer and social activist. Also see https://velivada.com/2017/09/03/dr-ambedkar-main-philosophy-women-empowerment/

3. Hindu Code Bill Section 14_Part_I

4. Arya, 2000: 63

CHAPTER IX

The Constitution of India and Women Rights

Source-:https://www.google.com/url?sa=i&url=https%3A%2F%2Fyouthincmag.com%2Fthe-indian-constitution-are-you-ignorant-or-informed-about-it&psig=AOvVaw1Dfc8Qu2CaFP8wU8A3UPPg&ust=1717918984608000&source=images&cd=vfe&opi=89978449&ved=0CBIQjRxqFwoTCIDii5DBy4YDFQAAAAAdAAAAABAQEnter Caption

Indian Constitution: Charter for Building an Equitable and Inclusive Society

The Indian Constitution is a charter for building an egalitarian and inclusive society which provides equal status to all and makes strong provisions to ensure a dignified life for all. Babasaheb Dr. Ambedkar, as the chief architect of the Constitution of India, established liberty, equality, fraternity, justice and personal dignity as the most valuable principles of the Constitution, which are the real jewels of a true democracy. Through the Indian Constitution, it has been fully ensured that every citizen of the country gets a life of dignity and respect without any discrimination on the basis of religion, caste, sex or place of birth.

Preamble of the Indian Constitution - Foundation of Equality and Justice

The Preamble of the Indian Constitution is a mirror of equality and social justice. It provides social, economic and political justice to all the citizens including women of India which is a sovereign, socialist, secular, democratic, republic. Every word of the Preamble has great importance and some of them are written in golden letters in our Constitution. There is no doubt in saying that the Preamble of the Indian Constitution reflects the basic values and principles necessary for social justice and establishes an egalitarian and inclusive social, economic and political culture in a country full of diversity.

The ideals and values cited in the Preamble set the goal of making the lives of men as well as women dignified. The Preamble shows that social, economic and political justice is not only for men, but also for women in the same form and proportion as for men. That is, the Constitution does not allow the government or any other authority to discriminate against women in the slightest way. All types of freedom and equality are necessary for women as well, through the Preamble and other provisions the Constitution has ensured that women get all the freedoms that men get. That is, by eliminating gender inequality, the principle of gender equality has not only been established but also measures have been taken to implement it with the power of law. The Preamble instructs the state to provide equal opportunities for progress to women as well. The preamble of the Indian constitution can be read as follows-

"We, the people of India, having solemnly resolved to constitute India into a sovereign socialist secular democratic republic and to secure to all its citizens social, economic and political justice;

liberty of thought, expression, belief, faith and worship;

equality of status and of opportunity;

and to promote fraternity assuring the dignity of the individual and the unity and integrity of the nation,

in this our Constituent Assembly on this the 26th day of November, 1949 (Mitti Margashirsha Shukla Saptami Samvat two thousand six Vikrami) do hereby adopt, enact and give ourselves this Constitution".

Fundamental Rights

Fundamental Rights: Protection of Gender Equality and Social Justice

Part III of the Indian constitution deals with fundamental rights which is the most important part related to social justice. The Indian constitution provides six fundamental rights to all citizens without any discrimination on the basis of caste, race, religion, sex and place of birth. These fundamental rights are not only for men, they are also given to women in equal form and in equal proportion. Similarly, the Constitution of India also provides full protection to women through fundamental rights. These are as follows:

1. Rights of the beneficiary (Articles 14 to 18)
2. Right to freedom (Articles 19 to 22)
3. Right against exploitation (Articles 23 to 24)
4. Right to religious freedom (Articles 25 to 28)
5. Cultural and fundamental rights (Articles 29 to 30)
6. Constitutional remedies (Article 32)

The fundamental rights mainly the right to equality (Articles 14-18) completely rejects the practice of inequality and discrimination on the basis of religion, sex, caste, race or place of birth and abolishes untouchability by creating equality among all citizens including women. It has been declared punishable by law in principle and practice. It ensures equal employment opportunities for women and men and prohibits discrimination by the state in matters of employment on the basis of caste, religion, etc.

Right to Freedom (Articles 19-22) is one of the most important ideals cherished by any democratic society that values the liberty of citizens. The Indian Constitution guarantees six types of freedom to citizens including women. The right to freedom includes several important rights such as:

- Freedom of speech and expression
- Freedom to assemble without arms
- Freedom of association
- Freedom to move freely within the country
- Freedom to reside and settle in any part of the territory of India
- Freedom to practice any profession

Right against Exploitation (Articles 23-24) prohibits human trafficking, beggary and other forms of forced labour. It also means prohibition of employment of children in factories etc. The constitution prohibits employment of children below 14 years of age in hazardous conditions.

Right to Freedom of Religion (Articles 25 - 28) not only grants religious freedom to all Indians including women but also indicates the secular nature of Indian politics. All religions are given equal respect here. It includes freedom of conscience, freedom to profess, practice and propagate any religion. Every person has the right freely to follow his faith, and to establish and maintain religious and charitable institutions.

Right to Constitutional Remedies under Article 32 is the most important as it provides a safeguard to all other rights. Therefore, Babasaheb Dr. Ambedkar called it the heart and soul of the constitution.

In this way, the Indian constitution has provided fundamental rights to men and women to live a life of respect and dignity. Dr. Ambedkar played an important role in getting these rights of India included in the Constitution of India. Indian women share these rights with male citizens in equal proportion without any discrimination and the credit for this mainly goes to Dr. Ambedkar.

It is worth mentioning here that women all over the world were deprived of the said rights and women had to struggle a lot for these rights. The said rights were not available to women in India too, but when Babasaheb Dr. Ambedkar got the responsibility of writing the Constitution of India, he unhesitantly gave all those rights to women as well which were given to men. That is, being the most powerful warrior of equality and social justice and a strong feminist thinker and activist, he ended the discrimination on the basis of gender that was going on for centuries through the Constitution and gave women an opportunity to live life with respect and dignity.

Directive Principles of State Policy

Protection of Women's Interests through Directive Principles of State Policy

Through the Directive Principles of State Policy (Articles 36 to 51) also, women's interests have been protected and the State has been directed to take special and qualified steps for the betterment of the weaker sections mainly women. Dr. Ambedkar was serious about the Directive Principles and its implementation. The Directive Principles ensure that the State shall strive to promote the welfare of the people by securing a social order in which justice, social, economic and political, pervades/informs all the institutions of life, as per Article 38(1).

- As per Article 38, the State shall strive to minimise the inequalities in income and endeavour to eliminate economic inequality as well as inequalities in status and opportunities, not only among individuals but also among groups of people residing in different areas or engaged in different fields.
- As per Article 39, the State shall aim at securing the right to an adequate means of livelihood for all citizens, both men and women, as well as equal pay for equal work for both men and women. So that all citizens, male and female, have equal rights to get adequate means of livelihood.

Provision of political rights of women

As far as political rights of women are concerned, Dr. Ambedkar not only advocated for political rights of women, but also granted all political rights to women from the very first day of implementation of the Constitution of India in 1950. Under the Indian Constitution (Article 325 and 326), women were also granted voting rights by not considering any person ineligible for inclusion in any electoral roll on the basis of religion, race, caste, sex or any of these. Whereas in developed countries, women got voting rights after a long struggle. US and UK granted voting rights to women in 1920 and 1928 respectively. Along with voting rights, women also have political rights to contest elections for any constitutional post and to hold any public office in the same proportion as men.

Impact of Indian Constitution: Women in various public positions

However, women have not yet got proper representation in the political field. But still, as a result of the rights granted under the Constitution of India based on equality and social justice, various women have got the opportunity to adorn various public positions, a brief description of which is as follows:

Woman as The President of India

Out of the total 15 Presidents elected so far, Smt. Pratibha Devisingh Patil and Smt. Draupadi Murmu have reached the post of President of India. The current President Smt. Draupadi Murmu gave the credit of her reaching the post of President of India to Baba Saheb Dr. Ambedkar. Highlighting the outstanding contribution made by Dr. Ambedkar for women empowerment and the downtrodden and deprived society, President Smt. Draupadi Murmu, while speaking at the 10th Convocation of Babasaheb Bhimrao Ambedkar University (BBAU), Lucknow, said that Dr. Bhimrao Ambedkar is like God for her and it is because of him that she is here. She said it was a proud moment for her to address the students at the convocation ceremony of the university named after Baba Saheb. President Murmu said, "Dr. Bhimrao Ambedkar did something because of which I am standing before you today."[1]

Though India has elected 14 Vice-Presidents so far, not a single woman has become Vice-President, which is a matter of concern in terms of women participation.

Women Judges in the Supreme Court

The first woman judge in the Supreme Court was Fatima Beevi who was appointed on 6 October 1989. Since then, there have been 11 women judges in the court. Currently, out of the total 34 judges in the court (including the Chief Justice of India), 3 sitting* judges are women. However, no woman has been able to become Chief Justice of India (CJI) in the Supreme Court so far, which is a matter of concern and makes the female participation in the judiciary incomplete.

The list of women judges of the Supreme Court of India is as follows:

1. Fatima Biwi
2. Sujata Manohar
3. Ruma Pal
4. Gyan Sudha Mishra
5. Ranjana Desai
6. R. Bhanumathi
7. Indu Malhotra
8. Indira Banerjee
9. Hima Kohli*
10. Bela Trivedi*
11. B. V. Nagarathna*

Source[2]

Woman in the post of Prime Minister

Smt. Indira Gandhi has adorned the post of Prime Minister of India. However, one women has been appointed as a Prime Minister of the country. But it is very unpleasent to see that onle one women has raeched to the post of the PM. It is obvious to state that our politicians and political parties did not make serious efforts in this regard. These should make concrete efforts and come forward to work under women leadership. Women can lead the government and the nation as well as it had been shown by Mrs. Indira Gandhi.

Woman in the post of Speaker of Lok Sabha

Smt. Meera Kumar and Smt. Sumitra Mahajan have occupied the post of Speaker of the popular House of the Indian Parliament i.e. Lok Sabha.

Women Governors

Till now 24 women have adorned the post of Governor in various states of India. However, Sarojini Naidu was the first woman governor who had adorned this post in 1947 itself. Following are the 24 women who became governors of different states:

1. Sarojini Naidu
2. Padmaja Naidu
3. Vijayalakshmi Pandit
4. Sharda Mukherjee
5. Jothi Venkatachalam
6. Kumudben Joshi
7. Ram Dulari Sinha
8. Sarla Grewal
9. Sheila Kaul
10. Fatima Beevi
11. V. S. Ramadevi
12. Pratibha Devisingh Patil
13. Prabha Rau
14. Margaret Alva
15. Kamla Beniwal
16. Urmila Singh
17. Sheila Dixit
18. Mridula Sinha
19. Draupadi Murmu
20. Najma Heptulla
21. Anandiben Patel*
22. Baby Rani Maurya
23. Anusuiya Uikey*
24. Tamilisai Soundararajan*

Out of the above, 3 are currently also adorning the post of governor.[3]

Women who have become Lieutenant Governors

So far, five women have become Lieutenant Governors. All of them have been Lieutenant Governors of Puducherry. The women who have held the post of Lieutenant Governor are as follows:

1. Chandravati
2. Rajendra Kumari Bajpai
3. Rajni Roy
4. Kiran Bedi
5. Tamilisai Soundararajan

Women Chief Ministers

So far, 16 women have become Chief Ministers in India, which are as follows:

1. Mrs. Sucheta Kriplani, (Uttar Pradesh)
2. Mrs. Nandini Satpathy, (Odisha)
3. Mrs. Shashikala Kakodkar, (Goa)
4. Mrs. Anwara Taimur, (Assam)
5. Mrs. V.N. Janaki Ramachandran, (Tamil Nadu)
6. Kumari J. Jayalalithaa, (Tamil Nadu)
7. Kumari Mayawati, (Uttar Pradesh)
8. Mrs. Rajinder Kaur Bhattal, (Punjab)
9. Mrs. Rabri Devi, (Bihar)
10. Mrs. Sushma Swaraj, (Delhi)
11. Mrs. Sheila Dixit, (Delhi)
12. Mrs. Vasundhara Raje Scindia, (Rajasthan)
13. Kumari Uma Bharti, (Madhya Pradesh)
14. Kumari Mamata Banerjee, (West Bengal)
15. Mrs. Anandiben Patel, (Gujarat)
16. Mrs. Mehbooba Mufti, (Jammu Kashmir)

Source:[4]

Conclusion

Since, in the Constitution of India, along with the right to vote, women have the political right to contest elections for any constitutional post and hold any public office in the same proportion as men. This is the reason that two women, Smt. Pratibha Devi Singh Patil and the current President Smt. Draupadi Murmu, have been adorned with the top post in India, i.e. the post of President. No woman had ever been able to become the head of such a huge nation in the known history of India. But, the current Constitution of India, made under the chairmanship of Babasaheb Dr. Ambedkar, has paved the way for women to reach the top post from the bottom. Not only this, it is because of this Constitution that today Smt. Murmu, who belongs to the tribal community, has reached the post of President, which is a historic event. Not only this, a woman in the form of Smt. Indira Gandhi has also become the Prime Minister of the Republic of India, which is the most important post in the Indian governance system. Many women have occupied the posts of ministers in the central and state governments. Women have also become Chief Ministers in many states. This is the beauty of the current Constitution of India, which is completely an excellent document of equality and social justice. The credit for all this goes to Babasaheb Dr. Ambedkar who, through his struggles, sacrifices and intelligence, created a situation that seemed unbelievable and unimaginable.

References

1. https://www.hindustantimes.com/cities/lucknow-news/dr-ambedkar-is-like-god-to-me-president-murmu-at-bbau-convocation-101676311363362.html
2. https://en.wikipedia.org/wiki/List_of_female_judges_of_the_Supreme_Court_of_India
3. https://en.wikipedia.org/wiki/List_of_female_governors_and_lieutenant_governors_in_India#References
4. https://en.wikipedia.org/wiki/List_of_female_chief_ministers_in_India

CHAPTER X

Women Political Representation – 1952 to 2024

The world history proves the fact that women have always been considered as second class in comparison to men and there has been male-domination in every sphere of life in society as a whole and in particular. Women have always been denied proper opportunities in every sphere. In the feudal era, the position of women was extremely deplorable and they were treated as mere objects. In modern times, gender discrimination along with other discriminations was abolished in theory, but in practice women suffered discrimination and humiliation. Equality for women, both within and outside the family, remained a distant dream. In the modern era, the concept of democracy came into being in Europe and women got some respect and emancipation. However, they were not granted the right to vote. In the early stage of the 20th century, the right to vote was limited to men only and women were deprived of the right to vote.

Women's Suffrage in Democratic Countries

Movements demanding women's suffrage came into existence in democratic countries. As a result, the US granted women suffrage in 1920, followed by Britain in 1928. Switzerland, considered the land of democracy, offered women suffrage in 1971, which was much later than India. In 1893, New Zealand became the first country to allow women to vote by adopting the principle of universal adult suffrage. Women were given the right to vote on a universal and equal basis in Lebanon in 1952, Syria (to vote) in 1949, Egypt in 1956, Tunisia in 1959, Mauritania in 1961, Algeria in 1962. While Islamic countries like Morocco in 1963, Libya and Sudan in 1964, Yemen in 1967, Bahrain in 1973, Jordan in 1974, Iraq in 1980, Kuwait in 1985 (though later withdrawn and granted again in 2005), Oman in 1994 granted political rights to women including the right to vote.[1]

Suffrage to women in India

In India, as soon as the Indian Constitution, mainly drafted by Dr. Ambedkar, came into force, all men and women were granted the right to vote without any discrimination on the basis of caste, religion, sex etc. in 1950 itself. Undoubtedly, Dr. Ambedkar played an important role in getting women the right to vote. Here, it is worth noting that since Dr. Ambedkar was a strong egalitarian, he was also a strong feminist and wanted to empower women in every way. Therefore, along with the right to vote, other political rights were also given to women. Dr. Ambedkar had a huge contribution behind this. This was also necessary because after gaining independence from colonial rule, India became a democratic country and the right to vote holds great importance in a democratic country. Democracy cannot be imagined without the right to vote. It is in fact the soul of democracy, as it ensures the participation and representation of citizens in the political system of a democratic country. And no country can become a complete democracy without giving the right to vote to all citizens including women.

Provision of Women Reservation in Panchayati Raj Institutions and Urban Local Bodies

Efforts have been made to ensure their participation and representation at the grassroots level itself. In this regard, the 73rd and 74th amendments to the Constitution were made in 1992 to increase and ensure their representation in Panchayati Raj Institutions and Urban Local Bodies. These amendments provided one-third (1/3) representation to women in Gram Panchayats, Panchayat Samitis and Zila Parishads respectively at the rural level and in Nagarpalika Samiti (Nagar Samiti), Nagarpalika Parishad (Nagar Parishad) and Nagar Nigam (Nagar Nigam) at the urban level. Since 1992, millions of women have got a share in local self-governance. All this is due to India's constitution which is egalitarian, inclusive and based on social justice.

Representation of women in Lok Sabha

It has been observed that the electoral participation and representation of women in India was also not satisfactory. Due to male-domination, they lagged behind in terms of electoral representation. Even after more than 75 years of independence, they are almost deprived politically. In terms of electoral representation, their condition has been worse than the deprived as the Scheduled Castes (15%) and Scheduled Tribes (7.5%) get representation in the Lok Sabha according to their population ratio. However, it is the policy of reservation due to which SCs and STs are getting representation in the Parliament (under Article 330) and State Legislative Assemblies (Article 332).

The electoral data available since 1952 shows that the political condition of women has not been good and their role in electoral politics has been very minimal.

Year 1957

Female Candidates: 45
Female MPs : 22
Representation Percentage: 4.4
Year 1962
Female Candidates: 66
Female MPs : 31
Representation Percentage: 7.3
Year 1967
Female Candidates: 67
Female MPs : 29
Representation Percentage: 6.2
Year 1971
Female Candidates: 86
Female MPs : 21
Representation Percentage: 5.2
Year 1977
Female Candidates: 70
Female MPs : 19
Representation Percentage: 3.5
Year 1980
Female Candidates: 143
Female MPs : 28
Representation Percentage: 5.7
Year 1984
Female Candidates: 171
Female MPs : 43
Representation Percentage: 8.6.
Year 1989
Female Candidates: 198
Female MPs : 29
Representation Percentage: 5.9
Year 1991
Female Candidates: 330
Female MPs : 38
Representation Percentage: 7.7
Year 1996
Female Candidates: 599
Female MPs : 40

Representation Percentage: 7.7
Year 1998
Female Candidates: 274
Female MPs : 43
Representation Percentage: 8.3
Year 1999
Female Candidates: 284
Female MPs : 49
Representation Percentage: 9.4
Year 2004
Female Candidates: 355
Female MPs : 45
Representation Percentage: 8.7
Year 2009
Female Candidates: 556
Female MPs : 59
Representation Percentage: 10.7
Year 2014
Female Candidates: 668
Female MPs : 62
Representation Percentage: 11.6
Year 2019
Female Candidates: 716
Female MPs : 78
Representation Percentage: 14.6
Source–Scroll.in[2]
Year 2024**
Female Candidates: 797
Female MPs :74
Representation Percentage: 13.62

However, women have been elected to the Lok Sabha since the first general election in 1952. But their participation was negligible in proportion to their numbers. It was only in the 2009 Lok Sabha election that women representation touched the figure of 50 when 59 women members succeeded in winning the election. It was a record representation since 1952, when the first General Election was held. In the elections before 2009, the number of women Lok Sabha members remained below 50. In the 16th Lok Sabha elections, a record 62 (11.6 percent) women candidates were elected. However, the 17th Lok Sabha elections (2019) brought about an improvement in women's representation compared to the 2014 Lok Sabha. Out of the 716 women candidates who contested, 78 were elected, which is 14.6% of the lower house and the highest ever women representation. However, this is not a matter of much joy as this figure is much less than the 33% that women activists have been demanding for a long time. But the parties are not considering women reservation as a serious issue and this is extremely worrying as far as women's interests are concerned.

As far as the latest General Election to Lok Sabha is concerned, a total of 74 women (13.62) have won the Lok Sabha elections, which shows a slight dip from 78 elected in 2019. Of the total women MPs elected to the Lower House from across the country, West Bengal is leading with 11 female MPs. A total of 797 women candidates had contested the elections. This trend of reduction in women representation in the popular house ie Lok Sabha is a matter of grave concern. Women representation reduced despite Indian Parliament has passed the Women Reservation Bill that provides 33% representation to women in Lok sabha and state assemblies. However, this bill still has not been implimented. Yet, it shows the seriousness of the political parties as far as women representation is concerned. Both the leading political parties, BJP and Congress fielded 69 and 41 women candidates respectively. This is not satisfactory approach of the political parties towards women political representation.

Provision of Women Reservation in Parliament and Legislative Assemblies

Recently, the Narendra Modi-led BJP government passed the Women's Reservation Bill by calling a special session of Parliament. Both the Lok Sabha (LS) and Rajya Sabha (RS) passed the Women's Reservation Bill 2023 (128th Constitutional Amendment Bill) named 'Nari Shakti Vandan Act'. This bill reserves one-third of the seats in the Lok Sabha, State Legislative Assemblies and Delhi Legislative Assembly. It will also apply to the seats reserved for SC (Scheduled Caste) and ST (Scheduled Tribe) in the Lok Sabha and State Legislative Assemblies.

Background of Women's Reservation Bill

The discussion on the Women's Reservation Bill has been prevalent since the tenure of former Prime Minister Shri Atal Bihari Vajpayee in 1996. Since the then government did not have a majority, the bill could not get approval. Attempts to reserve seats for women have been made earlier as well, details of which are as follows:

1996: The first Women's Reservation Bill was introduced in Parliament.

1998 - 2003: The government introduced the bill on 4 occasions but failed.

2009: The government introduced the bill amidst opposition.

2010: The Union Cabinet passed the bill and the Rajya Sabha passed it.

2014: The bill was expected to be introduced in the Lok Sabha.

Need for Women's Reservation Bill

Electoral politics has also not remained untouched by male-domination. Men influenced the voting behaviour of women according to their preferences and deprived them of adequate representation in electoral politics. Undoubtedly, the Government of India and the state governments launched various schemes and plans towards the upliftment and empowerment of women. However, the governments and the legislators have not taken any serious and concrete steps to increase their representation and participation in the political arena.

Undoubtedly, the population of women is almost half of the total population, but their participation in the public spheres, especially in politics, is not even one-fourth. The electoral participation of women in India i.e. their representation in the Lok Sabha and the state assemblies has not been satisfactory. Due to male-domination, women kept lagging behind in terms of electoral representation. Even after more than 75 years of independence, they are politically almost deprived. In terms of electoral representation, their situation has been worse than the deprived. Therefore, it is the need of the hour to ensure their participation in decision making in governance and this was not possible without reservation. Thus, the present government has taken steps in this direction which has undoubtedly paved the way for women representation.

There are 82 women MPs in Lok Sabha (15.2%) and 31 women in Rajya Sabha (13%). While this number has increased significantly since the first Lok Sabha (5%), it is still very low compared to many countries. As per the recent UN Women data, Rwanda (61%), Cuba (53%), Nicaragua (52%) are the top three countries in women representation. Bangladesh (21%) and Pakistan (20%) are also ahead of India in terms of women representation.

Key features of the Women's Reservation Bill

• Reservation for women in the Lower House

• The Bill provides for the insertion of Article 330A in the Constitution, drawing from the provisions of Article 330, which provides for reservation of seats for SCs/STs in the Lok Sabha.

• The Bill provided that seats reserved for women may be allocated by rotation in different constituencies in the States or Union Territories.

• Of the seats reserved for SCs/STs, the Bill seeks to reserve one-third of the seats for women on a rotation basis.

• Reservation for women in State Legislative Assemblies:

• The Bill introduces Article 332A, which mandates reservation of seats for women in every State Legislative Assembly. Additionally, one-third of the seats reserved for SCs and STs must be allocated for women, and one-third of the total seats filled through direct election to the Legislative Assemblies must also be reserved for women.

• Reservation for women in the National Capital Territory of Delhi (new section in 239AA):

• Article 239AA of the Constitution grants special status to the Union Territory of Delhi as the national capital in respect of its administrative and legislative functioning.

• The Bill amends article 239AA(2)(b) accordingly and adds that laws made by Parliament shall apply to the National Capital Territory of Delhi.

• Introduction of reservation (new article - 334A):

• The reservation will take effect after the publication of the census to be held after the coming into force of this Bill. Delimitation will be carried out to reserve seats for women on the basis of the census.

• The reservation will be provided for a period of 15 years. However, it will continue until such date as may be determined by law made by Parliament.

• Rotation of seats: The seats reserved for women will be rotated after each delimitation, as determined by law made by Parliament.[3]

Criticism of the Women Resevation Bill

The Bill only states that it "shall come into force after taking relevant figures for the first census after the commencement of the delimitation exercise for this purpose." It does not specify the cycle of elections that will give women their fair share. The Bill has been criticised on several counts, chiefly that its benefits are not immediate. It will be implemented only after constituency delimitation which may take a long time. The second reason for criticism is the disregard for social justice. The parties in favour of social justice demanded that the participation of women from OBC category should also be ensured in this women reservation. The critics argued that this law will benefit only women from urban and upper castes and women from backward communities will be left behind. Therefore, for the representation of women from OBC category, they are demanding quota within quota which also seems appropriate.

The present bill does not provide for reservation for women in Rajya Sabha and State Legislative Councils. At present, the representation of women in Rajya Sabha is even less than in Lok Sabha. Through this bill, reservation was arranged only in Lok Sabha and Legislative Assemblies of the states which cannot be called complete. Representation is an ideal which should be reflected in both the lower and upper houses. In a way, incomplete justice has been given to women by not ensuring representation of women in the upper houses. But still it can be said that this is a great beginning which was long awaited and the effort to ensure political participation of women after 76 years of independence is really a commendable step. However, in practical terms this reservation has not been implemented yet and it will have to wait for a long time. Women will not be able to get the benefit of this reservation in the upcoming 2024 Lok Sabha elections.

Conclusion

Undoubtedly, India had provided this most valuable right to women from the beginning of its democracy. However, it has been observed that they did not use it according to their wish. Their voting behavior was influenced and dominated by the will of men. This was the characteristic of the male-dominated attitude of the society. In Indian society, women had to live under the dominance of men from birth to death. They lived under the dominance of their fathers and brothers during childhood and youth. After marriage they lived under the dominance of their husbands and sons. Certainly, Babasaheb Dr. Ambedkar has played an important role directly and indirectly in the matter of political empowerment of women. Despite this, their political backwardness continued. The main reason for this was the male-dominated mindset of the society. Even educated women did not vote against the choice of male members of their family. This was the reason why they lagged behind men in terms of political participation and representation.

This shows that the condition of women in Indian democracy has not been satisfactory in terms of their political participation. Their representation in the country's parliament has been very low. Due to male-domination, they lagged behind in all spheres of life including political representation, which has been very close to the underprivileged sections of society. However, India has seen female Prime Minister Indira Gandhi, some ministers and chief ministers. But, the success of some women cannot be considered a yardstick to measure the representation of all women. They cannot determine the level of representation of all women. Thus, it seems inevitable to ensure the participation and representation of women, who constitute almost half of the country's population, in electoral politics. This is why for the last few years, the need to provide 33 percent reservation to women in Parliament, Legislative Assemblies and other law-making bodies was being emphasized across the country.

References

1. wikipedia

2. https://www.karnataka.com/elections/women-in-the-lok-sabha-since-independence/

3. https://www.drishtiias.com/daily-updates/daily-news-analysis/women-s-reservation-bill-2023

**https://www.ndtv.com/india-news/lok-sabha-election-results-2024-74-women-won-lok-sabha-polls-this-time-slight-dip-from-78-elected-in-2019-5826172

CHAPTER XI

Concluding Remarks: Dr. Ambedkar, a Great Visionary and a True Champion of Women Emancipation & Empowerment

It can be firmly said that along with the remarkable efforts made by Mahatma Jyotiba Phule, Savitribai Phule and Fatima Sheikh for girl education and women empowerment, the contribution of Baba Saheb Dr. B.R. Ambedkar has not only been extremely valuable and meaningful, but also most decisive. Dr. Ambedkar emerged as a true pioneer of women empowerment, who as a visionary strongly protected the interests of women and advocated equality and freedom for them. He had a great vision for the liberation and empowerment of women. Dr. Ambedkar's vision to women upliftment was very clear and amazing which also proves him to be a true feminist thinker and philosopher. Along with fighting for the rights of downtrodden and backward classes, he also raised his voice strongly for the interests of women. When he got the opportunity to make the Constitution of India, he took special steps to ensure the liberation and empowerment of women as the chief architect of the Constitution. By making a constitution based on equality, he also gave a concrete form to gender equality and without considering women inferior in any way, he gave full encouragement to the dignity of women and their progress.

As far as women liberation and girl education are concerned, Dr. Ambedkar was greatly influenced by his father Ramji Sakpal who never discriminated against his daughters and taught them at home. He was very keen on women's education even at a time when girl education was considered a sin and against religion. Mahatma Jyotiba Phule who is considered to be the political guru of Dr. Ambedkar and his wife Savitribai Phule also influenced him a lot in the matter of women education and empowerment. They made very commendable and serious efforts for women empowerment and were successful to a great extent in liberating women from the shackles of slavery.

Dr. Ambedkar was a natural supporter of girl child education and women empowerment. He was the first Indian to break the barriers in the way of advancement of women in India as he laid the foundation of concrete and sincere efforts by codifying the common code for Hindus and other sections of Indian society. Dr. Ambedkar's proposals were later passed in four bills on Hindu 'Marriage', 'Inheritance', 'Minority and Guardianship' and 'Maintenance'. But in spite of constitutional and legal safeguards, women are not getting the freedom and rights that the male citizens of the country are enjoying. Still they seem to be subjected to subjugation, exploitation and humiliation. Constitutionally and legally they have been given equal rights as human beings but in reality they are deprived of rights through social, economic and religious mechanisms. Yet they are struggling for adequate representation in the legislatures of the country and the states. As far as the political status of women is concerned, they still lag behind their male counterparts.

As far as women empowerment is concerned, Dr. Ambedkar's contribution has been of pioneering nature. To elevate the social, economic and political status of women, Dr. Ambedkar stressed on education which was one of his three great ideas - "Educate, Unite and Agitate". Undoubtedly, it is the result of the great efforts of feminists like Dr. Ambedkar that women could come into the public sphere and are playing their amazing roles in the field of politics and public services. Now they can become rulers, legislators, judges, professors, journalists, civil servants, police officers, doctors, engineers, pilots etc.

Dr. Ambedkar emerged as a true champion of women empowerment who strongly defended the interests of women and supported their equality and freedom. Along with fighting for the rights of the underprivileged, he also raised a vibrant voice for women. As far as women's liberation and girl child education are concerned, he was greatly influenced by his father Ramji Sakpal, who never discriminated against his daughters and taught them at home. He was very keen on women's education even in those times when girl child education was considered a sin and against religion.

He laid the foundation for solid and honest efforts by codifying the common code for Hindus and other sections of Indian society. He said that women should be given all-round development for social education, their well-being and socio-cultural rights. He emphasized that each section of Indian women should be given their due share and it is necessary to maintain and protect the dignity and modesty of women. He made basic provisions in the constitution to secure the rights of women in the constitution. He tried his best to free women from age-old rotten traditions and ensure a respectable and dignified life for them through the Hindu Code

Bill.

In fact, as a warrior of equality, freedom, fraternity and justice, Dr. Ambedkar was such a strong supporter of women empowerment that for the sake of women's interests and rights, he even resigned from the post of Law Minister of the Government of India. Such a great feminist thinker and such a serious well-wisher of women will hardly be found in India. All the women of India should keep this in mind. But it is a matter of regret that Dr. Ambedkar is known more as the leader of Dalits only, in the true sense he was also a very serious well-wisher of half the population of the country i.e. women.

There is no doubt that it is the result of the great efforts of Dr. Ambedkar that since 1950 women are participating in the public sector and playing their amazing role in the field of education, literature, science, journalism, politics, security and civil services, whereas before independence their participation in these fields was almost negligible. Now they are adorning the positions of rulers, ministers, MPs, MLAs, judges, professors, journalists, civil servants, police officers, doctors, engineers, pilots etc. Since, in the Constitution of India, along with the right to vote, women have the same political rights to contest elections for any constitutional post and to hold any public post as men. This is the reason that two women, namely Mrs. Pratibha Devi Singh Patil and the current President Mrs. Draupadi Murmu, have been adorned with the top post in India, i.e. the post of President.

No woman had ever been able to become the head of such a huge nation in the known history of India. But, the current Constitution of India, made under the chairmanship of Babasaheb Dr. Ambedkar, has paved the way for women to reach the top post from the bottom. Not only this, it is because of this Constitution that today Mrs. Murmu, who belongs to the tribal community, has reached the post of President, which is a historic event. Not only this, a woman in the form of Mrs. Indira Gandhi has also become the Prime Minister of the Republic of India, which is the most important post in the Indian governance system. Many women have occupied the posts of ministers in the central and state governments. Women have also become Chief Ministers in many states. This is the beauty of the present Constitution of India which is a wonderful document of complete equality and social justice. The credit for all this goes to Babasaheb Dr. Ambedkar who, through his struggles, sacrifices and wisdom, created a situation that seemed unbelievable and unimaginable.

Today, their power and participation in society is constantly increasing and they are enjoying equal freedoms and rights with men. The reason for this is the Constitution written by Babasaheb Dr. Ambedkar which not only provides equal rights to women and men but also prohibits discrimination against women on the basis of gender. Not only this, the present Constitution of India also issues instructions to the state and government to take necessary and concrete steps for the upliftment and empowerment of women. In fact, the real credit for women empowerment goes to Dr. Ambedkar who was truly a great warrior of equality, freedom, fraternity and social justice in India.

According to Dr. Vikas Divyakirti, the heartbeat of the youth who aspire to become civil servants and a well-known teacher of Drishti Coaching Center in Delhi, "Some people consider Dr. Ambedkar as the leader of the Scheduled Castes only. He further said that all the girls sitting here (in the class), especially Hindu girls, should offer a flower to his statue every day. If Ambedkar was not there, you would have been doing household chores. Ambedkar has done as much good work for the liberation of Hindu women as no one else has done together."*

Undoubtedly, women should be grateful to Babasaheb Dr. Ambedkar and should always remember him as the liberator of women. Along with this, women should also be aware of their legal and constitutional rights and should be constantly vigilant, only then they will be able to use their rights and protect these rights for which Babasaheb Dr. Ambedkar fought hard and contributed a lot. Otherwise these rights can be limited by conservative and religious forces, who have ill intentions towards the rights of women and against whom Dr. Ambedkar fought to get these rights for women. Indeed, Babasaheb Dr. B.R. Ambedkar was a great visionary and a true champion of women liberation and empowerment

Reference

*https://www.youtube.com/watch?v=TUT2Q17XR_M

About The Author

Dr. Kuldeep Singh: The Author of this book

Dr. Kuldeep Singh is presently working as Senior Lecturer of Political Science under Haryana Education Department at Government Adarsh Sanskriti Senior Secondary School, Sector-55, Faridabad. He has earned many degrees such as graduation (B.A. Hons.-Political Science), post graduation (M.A.), PG Diploma in Dalit and Minorities Studies and Ph.D. in Political Science from Jamia Millia Islamia a central university, New Delhi. He qualified the NET examination conducted by UGC in June 1998 in Political Science subject. He has authored five books, two chapters in an edited book and 8 Articles in various national journals.

Author's Other Published Works (*Books* and Articles)

1. Dr. Vijay Kumaar Varma edt. *Gandhi aur Samakaaleen Vishva* (Pinnacle Learning, New Delhi) one chapter, "bhaarat mein krshak satyaagrah"

2. Dr. Vijay Kumaar Varma edt. *Gandhi aur Samakaaleen Vishva* (Pinnacle Learning, New Delhi) one chapter, "mandir pravesh evan jaativaad ka virodh

3. *Electoral Politics Of India: Emerging Trends*, Lambert Academic Publishing, Germany, 2011

4. *INDIAN WARRIORS OF EQUALITY AND SOCIAL JUSTICE*, Notion Press, Chennai, 2022 (ISBN-9798888492253)

5. *BHARAT ME SAMAJIK NYAY KI AAWAJ*: Dr. Ambedkar tatha Anay Purodhaon ka Sangharsh evam Yogdan, Notion Press, Chennai, 2023 (ISBN-13 : 979-8890266088)

6. *HARYANA POLITICS ISSUES AND TRENDS SINCE 1991*, Notion Press, Chennai, 2023

7. *MAHILA ADHIKAARON KE LIYE DR. AMBEDKAR KA YOGADAAN*, Notion Press, Chennai, 2023 (ISBN-0000000496987)

8. Reservation: An Issue of Controversy in Contemporary India, Punjab Journal of Politics, vol. 31, 2007 (Article)

9. Dalit Politics and Leadership after Dr. B.R. Ambedkar, IJSW, TISS, Mumbai, 2009 (Article)

10. Violation of Human Rights Some Observation in Haryana, IJSW, TISS, Mumbai, 2013 (Article)

11. Dynasty in Indian Politics: A Study Focusing Haryana State, MPJSS, Vol. 18, June 2013 (Article)

12. Women' Political Participation: A Study Referring Haryana Assembly Elections, JPS, vol. XI, November 2015 (Article)

13. Employment, Government Recruitments and Politics: A Study, MPJSS, Vol. 20, December 2015 (Article)

14. Caste and Politics: A Study in Perspective of Socio-Economic Survey-2011, JPS, Vol. 13, April-2017 (Article)

15. India's 17th Lok Sabha General Elections, 2019: Electoral Continuity and Change, IJCRT, Voulme 12, issue 2 February 2024/ISSN: 2320-2882

www.ingramcontent.com/pod-product-compliance
Lightning Source LLC
LaVergne TN
LVHW021200160826
845679LV00024B/2181

* 9 7 9 8 8 9 5 1 9 6 0 8 3 *